Praise for

THE COMMUNAL HEART

"*The Communal Heart* by Claudia Dommaschk is a groundbreaking work that plants seeds of liberation in the collective imagination. It is a rare and necessary book—one that speaks directly to the ache of our times. With exquisite clarity and mythic sensitivity, Claudia maps how we move from isolation to belonging, from collapse to coherence, from the fractured self to a shared pulse that feels both ancient and radically new. This is not merely a book about community; it is a blueprint for rehumanization. Every page beats with insight, courage, and a fierce tenderness for what we are capable of becoming together. Few writers can hold complexity with such grace—fewer still can translate it into frameworks that feel both intellectually rigorous and soulfully alive. *The Communal Heart* is required reading for anyone who cares about the future of our shared humanity and seeks a new way forward. It's one of the clearest, strongest, and most transformative works in the space of non-religious spirituality."

—JIM PALMER, Author of *Notes from (Over) the Edge*,
and Founder of Center for Non-Religious Spirituality

"Most books about belonging are written from within the fragmentation they claim to diagnose. Dommaschk has done the harder thing: she's written from integration, which means the structure of the book performs what the content describes. This is what genuine metamodern work looks like in practice."

—EMIL EJNER FRIIS, co-author of *The Listening Society*

"*The Communal Heart* is a timely call back to belonging within ourselves and with one another. Claudia Dommaschk weaves Gestalt insight, somatic wisdom, and grounded practice into a clear invitation toward the communal coherence our world is asking of us."

—STEVEN HARPER, Psychologist, Gestalt Practitioner, and Workshop Leader of the Esalen Institute

"Claudia's work is a potent reminder of just how far we can go if we slow down enough to collectively rediscover our communal heart. She's an active trailblazer in the field of community weaving, and her first book has eloquently laid out a pathway towards that most rare and sacred of things...sustained relational resonance! We need so much more of what Claudia's doing in the world, and I sleep better at night knowing she's out there leading the way. Her words shine forth with a mother's love, a therapist's keen insight, and a practitioner's hard-won wisdom. This book is for everyone who's genuinely ready to belong."

—JOE LIGHTFOOT, Author of *A Collective Blooming: The Rise of Mutual Aid Community*

"In this beautiful book, Claudia Dommaschk's writing unfolds like a watercolor painting, layer by layer, revealing a path that comes gradually into view. And somewhere along the way, something in us softens and recognizes itself. The heart responds with a quiet 'yes'—a felt sense that, beneath the surface, belonging has always been true."

—LUCIE CHALIFOUR, Spiritual Director/Childbirth Educator and Founder of Unfolding New Life

"Dommaschk has a rare gift: rigorous models that you can actually feel your way into. Again and again, she finds the counterintuitive angle on material that could easily have been predictable. Essential reading for anyone who leads people."

—ROBERT KELLEY AYALA, Managing Director of VIBE LABS

" In this book, Claudia Dommaschk presents us with a systemic analysis of the forces pulling us apart, which is a great step in our healing journey. She also offers us an evolutionary path to transform our individual selves and to use relational intelligence to create loving relationships and wisdom communities, thus contributing to a better world."

—MANUEL MANGA, Founder and Director of the Center for Evolutionary Leadership

"This is a beautiful book as it will hold you, entrance you, and activate what's within us all. However, it's far more practical and powerful than this—merely coming home to ourselves. Our boundaries don't stop there; what matters is between us and among us—taking us into the fractals of coherence—our awareness, sensing, and feeling, changes the world."

—SIMON DIVECHA, Ph.D., Founder of Soulsentient

"*The Communal Heart* carries a timely message on the connections we've lost, the toll this loss has taken, and why a return to community will be a critical part of our individual and collective journeys back toward wholeness. Perhaps even more importantly, Claudia shows us how to find and nurture the connections we've all been looking for."

—JEFF WILLIAMS, Co-founder of Network of Networks

"In *The Communal Heart*, Claudia Dommaschk brings us back to something ancient and essential: the relational intelligence of the heart. Both a clear-eyed diagnosis of our cultural fracture and a compelling path toward repair, this is a book for anyone seeking to meet the crises of our time without losing their humanity."

—GOD'SWILL OSA, Ph.D. in Government,
Writer of Politics and Embodiment

"As the metacrisis deepens, the need for healthy masculine energy supporting healthy feminine energy grows. It is time for the Queen and her Knights. In *The Communal Heart*, Claudia Dommaschk shows us a way. Her book is special to me because she is a dear friend. It is now my intention to direct some of my masculine energy towards supporting the healthy feminine energy evident in Claudia's book."

—JOHN STOKDIJK, a founding member of Wisdom
Exchange, an international community committed
to making sense of a complex world.

The COMMUNAL HEART

The COMMUNAL HEART

A RETURN TO BELONGING IN A WORLD PULLING US APART

CLAUDIA DOMMASCHK

WONDERWELL PRESS

Published by Wonderwell Press
Austin, Texas
www.gbgpress.com

Distributed by Greenleaf Book Group

For ordering information or special discounts for bulk purchases, please contact Greenleaf Book Group at PO Box 91869, Austin, TX 78709, 512.891.6100.

Design and composition by Greenleaf Book Group and Sheila Parr
Cover design by Greenleaf Book Group and Sheila Parr
Cover images used under license from Adobe Stock:
69637460 / undrey; 878713108 / CreativeVista

Publisher's Cataloging-in-Publication data is available.

Print ISBN: 978-1-963827-46-0

eBook ISBN: 978-1-963827-47-7

To offset the number of trees consumed in the printing of our books, Greenleaf donates a portion of the proceeds from each printing to the Arbor Day Foundation. Greenleaf Book Group has replaced over 50,000 trees since 2007.

Printed in the United States of America on acid-free paper

26 27 28 29 30 31 32 33 10 9 8 7 6 5 4 3 2 1

First Edition

To those who come after us

CONTENTS

PREFACE

Ours is not the task of fixing the entire world at once, but of stretching out to mend the part of the world that is within our reach.

—*Clarissa Pinkola Estés*

I did not set out to write this book.

Writing came to me quietly, in the whispers of my soul, in the hush before sunrise, in the last flickers of daylight. In the liminal space between what has been and what longs to emerge is where this book found its breath.

Finding our voice is one of the most sacred acts of being alive. I have been searching for mine for a while, first in the echoing halls of a lonely childhood home and later in academic corridors where intellect was prized over intuition. Often, I spoke in the hope of being understood. When that bridge of understanding faltered, I learned to steady myself on uncertain ground by leaning toward abstraction, linearity, and what seemed expected. I tried to craft responses that were polished, abstract, and clear.

But this time, writing itself has changed me.

With a stronger sense of myself, I am trusting my inner voice, allowing it to move through me less filtered and more alive. It now arises from a place that feels both uniquely mine yet profoundly shared. It unfolds in spirals rather than straight lines. It holds me as much as I hold it. In this movement, it reveals an important truth: How we speak is part of what we say. The structure of a message is never separate from its flow.

You may wonder why a book on healing would begin with a personal disclosure about process, or why emergence is worth considering at all.

Healing is not only about addressing the content of the wound itself. It is also about contact, presence, and the quality of the attention we bring to the wound. True healing asks us to unravel the stories threaded into the wound and to listen for what longs to be born through it.

I imagine you agree. Something is unraveling among us. We feel the tension in our bodies, in our relationships, and in the anxiety that hums beneath the surface of everyday life. The ways we commonly live, driven by domination and marked by disconnection, no longer hold. We have outgrown them, or perhaps, they have outworn us. Either way, the center of our modern society seems to be collapsing. Yet amid this unraveling, something else, more vital, is beginning to break through.

This book emerges from this place where the personal and cultural meet, not in theory, but in the lived experience of watching well-thought-out strategies and carefully constructed systems fail. Meanwhile, the human spirit persists, courageously insisting on another way, on another process.

As a psychotherapist, I have sat beside people when they were most unguarded, as old narratives fall away and new ones begin to form. I have come to recognize that what we are experiencing, as modern human beings, shaped by Western ideals of progress and individuality, is not merely a psychological reckoning, but a spiritual, ecological, and civilizational shift.

We are standing together on a threshold.

When I reflect on this realization, the implications become clear. Our crisis is not just political, economic, or environmental. It is also relational. We have lost connection with our bodies, with one another, with what is sacred, and with the deeper intelligence that exists in all things. We have been trained to relate to this intelligence from fear and through the pressure to perform and be productive. We have been sold an illusion of control, and it is harming us.

But the truth is, we can remember another way. Remembering how to be with one another, how to listen, how to love without an agenda, is the foundation for returning to a relational field of connection that exists within us, between us, and among us. This field of relationship longs to be restored.

While this book is, in part, a diagnosis, it is primarily a call to acknowledge what is breaking and to begin the slow work of mending. It is not about fixing the world through smarter strategies. It is about reclaiming what makes us human and expanding our capacity to witness, feel, and relate across difference without collapsing into division.

I offer this book as a response to the commodification of our inner lives and the exhaustion so many of us carry from trying to find our place in a culture that has forgotten the essential need for belonging. Within these pages, I map the pervasive forces that pull us apart and offer an embodied return, one that invites both personal healing and a renewed capacity to find coherence with one another.

Because healing, genuine healing, does not happen in isolation. It happens in communion.

If you have been feeling that something is not right but cannot quite name it, if you have longed for a different kind of leadership but are not sure what it looks like, or if you have sensed that a collective reorientation is underway but do not know how to participate in it, consider this the signal that you are remembering another way.

So, let us begin right where we are, in the space between what is breaking down and what is subtly breaking through. Let us cultivate relational practices that honor difference, welcome resonance, and make room for the full spectrum of becoming. What ultimately enables us to grow and flourish is not the path we choose, but whether it brings us closer to who we truly are.

Our shared future depends on this.

Davis, California
May 2026

Introduction

THE HEART WE HAVE FORGOTTEN

The future belongs to those who give the
next generation reason for hope.
—Pierre Teilhard de Chardin

In a twist that sounds more like science fiction than social research, an April 2025 *Forbes* article by John Koetsier reported that over 80 percent of Gen Z users who engage with AI chatbots said, if given the choice, they would marry their bots over a real person.[1] I nearly waved it off as another strange footnote in our rapidly evolving technological landscape, but when I paused to reflect, the implications became sobering. People aren't falling in love with machines because they don't know better. They're reaching for what they can no longer reliably find elsewhere.

For younger generations, those learning to love and connect by watching adults around them who are themselves increasingly absorbed by screens, this blurring of emotional boundaries between humans and machines is especially disorienting. As a tech-driven society, we seem to be choosing intimacy without the raw messiness of human relationships. In a world where real connections have grown increasingly strained, it is no surprise that AI offers a more comforting, predictable alternative.

But let's be clear: These "relationships" are simulations.

Why are we willing to trade real, embodied connection for a curated facsimile? If the contentment we draw from these simulated relationships isn't merely about a technological fascination, then perhaps this longing points to a far more serious concern. I believe it does.

Everywhere we look, systems are under stress. We're inundated with reports of climate collapse, economic inequality, a loneliness epidemic, and increasing polarization.[2] What we're witnessing isn't a series of isolated crises but the culmination of a long, slow unraveling of relational life.

At the heart of this unraveling—what many now refer to as the metacrisis or a crisis of crises—is a breakdown in how we relate to ourselves, one another, the Earth, and the mysterious pulse of life that animates it all.[3] Shaped by a modern culture that privileges competition over compassion, dominance over dialogue, and certainty over curiosity, we seem to have forgotten how to be with one another in ways that nourish and sustain us. As our relationships fray, so too does the fabric of our shared existence.

To begin healing these cultural divides, this book explores the fragmentation in perception and meaning-making that distorts how we engage, both within ourselves and with the world around us. Together, we will examine the gendered and social fissures that shape how we live, lead, and love, as well as the widening rift between humans and the natural world. Our aim is to understand and repair the disconnection that severs us from the very ground of our belonging.

As a psychotherapist, wife, mother, and lifelong student of personal transformation and community-building initiatives, including Wisdom Exchange, I've spent many hours listening to people, observing patterns, and holding the silent spaces in between that carry countless untold stories.[4] During this time, I've come to realize that much of our suffering begins with ruptures in relationships. The feeling of being unseen and unsafe, or the belief that vulnerability is a weakness, often stems from our earliest childhood experiences and is reinforced throughout life. These formidable wounds affect how we move through the world and, in turn, how we relate to it. When disconnection becomes our default, it is present in all aspects of our lives. It appears in the private pain and invisible struggles we feel compelled to carry alone, unsure of how to ask for support or whether it would even be safe to do so. It also shows up in the ideologies we cling to, where fear replaces wonder and opposing views become threats rather than opportunities for understanding. And it becomes evident in our growing difficulty collaborating across differences, as trust erodes and we forget how to listen, negotiate, and coordinate together.

And yet, there is another way. I've also witnessed the unmistakable power of reconnection, moments when defenses soften, and tenderness becomes a bridge rather than a threat. Such moments are not only personally healing but also collectively transformative. When one heart opens, it invites others to do the same. This positive effect ripples outward, touching the person who experiences it and the web of relationships they are a part of.

This book is a path of return.

Drawing on over thirty years of working with clients to cultivate connection, alongside my study of psychotherapy and my lived experience, I offer an integrated path that invites us to move courageously toward the fractures of modern life and begin mending the field that holds us together. I call this field of interconnected relationships—this dynamic realm of relationality—the Communal Heart.[5]

Because your time and attention are precious, I attempt to share this path into the Communal Heart with humility and care. Across five parts, this book introduces you to a way of reentering the field of belonging, a term we'll become more familiar with later, that begins with presence, deepens through mutuality, and draws its strength from coherence. It is an invitation to remember what connects us, restore what has been forgotten, and reclaim the aliveness that emerges when we meet life and one another as we are.

Each chapter welcomes you into the ideas and then accompanies you in bringing them into practice. To help ground the material in lived experience, you'll encounter real-life stories with all identifying details, including names and quotes, carefully changed to protect the privacy of those involved. I also draw on my clinical work, personal experience, and an ongoing dialogue with the cultural threshold we are all living through to share philosophical insights, embodied practices, and reflective questions. My hope is that these offerings provide a shift not only within us as individuals but also among us as a people, helping us remember how to cohere again.

FINDING OUR WAY INTO SHARED MEANING

Much of the confusion and conflict we face today arises not only from seeing different facts but from inhabiting different perceptual worlds as well. The way we attend to life shapes what we can perceive. When attention narrows without a felt sense of context or relationship, reality can appear fragmented, objectified, and flat. When attention widens, a more relational and contextual world comes into view, one that includes tone, meaning, history, and possibility. These are not merely differences of opinion, but differences in modes of attention, each revealing a different kind of reality. How we attend, both in what we notice and in the quality of presence we bring, quite literally gives rise to the kind of world that shows up for us.

Throughout this book, I make careful distinctions between awareness, attention, mode of attention, and perception because these differences carry weight. Awareness refers to the spacious field in which experience unfolds. Attention is the movement within that field, the way we focus by widening or narrowing the scope of our engagement. When our mode of attention shifts, our mode of perception shifts with it. We do not just think differently; we *see* differently. Learning to work with attention, rather than being unconsciously driven by it, opens the possibility of more coherent perception, deeper relationships, and wiser responses.

Before we continue, let's explore the core theme that underlies this book. It centers on sensitive topics in biology and gender and on how social conditioning can confine our full expression as human beings. I imagine that what follows may stir emotion. Any perspective, including my own, presented here in this book, is partial and incomplete. My hope is that by bringing greater depth and care to the conversation, we might move toward a wider synthesis, not a definitive solution, but a meaningful step toward easing a long-standing tension between gender and culture in the modern world.

That said, I would like to clarify a few key terms, since arriving at a shared understanding of language is essential. Language can both illuminate and reduce. When we collapse people into labels, we risk objectifying them, turning living, breathing complexity into simplified categories. While labels can make conversation cognitively easier, they can also erase nuance and difference. When nuance is lost, so is mutuality. With this in mind, I offer the following definitions as working agreements, stepping stones toward a conversation that aims toward fuller understanding.

When I refer to "male" and "female," I'm speaking about biological sex—more specifically, the reproductive systems and secondary sex characteristics that give rise to sperm and egg, and through their union, to new life. When I use the words "man" and "woman," I am referring to those whose gender identity aligns with their biological sex, in other words, cisgender individuals. When I speak of "masculine" and "feminine," I'm not referring to fixed identities or traditional gender roles, but to general patterns of perception and participation found across cultures and stories over time, tendencies with biological roots that also live within each of us.[6] From this energetic standpoint, I understand the archetypal feminine as a mode of generative receptivity and relational attunement, and the archetypal masculine as a mode of penetrating focus and instrumental agency.[7]

While many examples in this book are informed by my work as a licensed marriage and family therapist with cisgender, heterosexual couples in the United States—contexts in which these general dynamics often appear in especially clear relief—the principles explored here are not confined to these pairings. They speak to a universal aspect of our shared humanity. It is in this spirit that I invite you to approach these dynamics not as prescriptions of gender identity or sexual orientation, but as expressions of relational energy that move through all human connections and much of the non-human world. My intention is to honor the diversity of lived experience while offering these reflections as openings into a deeper understanding of connection, rather than as limitations or fixed categories.

To support the integration of these insights into your relationships, communities, and professional life, you'll find guidelines for starting your own Wisdom Circle, along with a glossary of terms, at the end of the book. These additions are given as direction-finders to help you orient yourself as we navigate this emerging relational terrain together. At times, the book may be prescriptive, but it is not intended to be a manual. It is a map written in the language of relationship. More importantly, it is an invitation to open, listen, and trust what you already sense deep down: We were never meant to do this courageous and tender work alone.

As we walk this path into the Communal Heart, we begin to recover wholeness, not as an abstract ideal, but as a lived reality. In rediscovering the threads of connection that make life meaningful, we find our way home—home to ourselves, to one another, and to a world we belong to, one that, in its subtle way, longs to belong to us too.

THE SUPPORT AND INFLUENCES BEHIND THE WORK

Because the journey ahead is one of integration, it's important to share the thinkers and practitioners who have shaped my understanding and experience of relationality. More than mentors or guides, they are companions on this path, whether I met them in person or on the page.

Carl Jung offered an enduring foundation for my work, teaching me to recognize the psyche as a living, symbolic reality and to understand integration as an ongoing practice of holding opposites in relationship. Iain McGilchrist's insights into the divided brain deepened this understanding by revealing how our overidentification with narrow, abstract attention has pulled us away from wholeness, both personally and collectively. Dick Price and the lineage of Gestalt Practice taught me to trust emergence and to listen for what wants to come forward. Hanzi Freinacht's framework of metamodernism and Ken Wilber's integrative approach helped name the developmental pivot we're living through as a culture. Finally, Russ Hudson's interpretation of the Enneagram illuminated the sacred longing within me to come home to myself, others, and life itself. As someone who identifies with Point Four on the Enneagram, I have come to appreciate the joy and heartache of awakening to the freedom of reality through recognizing its artistic nature and profound depth. It is through these convergences, and sitting with people in the raw, unfinished places of their becoming, that my life's work, contained within these pages, comes forth.

Throughout the book, you may notice a recurring rhythm: "not just this, but also that," or "not only this, but that as well." You'll also come across occasional sentence fragments. These aren't mistakes or simply stylistic flourishes; they're intentional. They reflect a way of thinking and relating that resists closure in favor of curiosity, a rhythm that pauses to breathe and allows meaning to emerge slowly in its own time. This is more than a literary choice. The way we shape language mirrors how we move in the world. When we write and live this way, we begin to embrace nuance, hold tension, and honor the fertile space between polarities. Everything arises from this place and ultimately returns to it.

The structure of this book reflects the relational paradigm it seeks to evoke, one that values mutuality and generativity alongside individuation and self-realization. It calls us to reawaken our relational intelligence and meet the world not only as individuals but also as midwives and stewards of coherence. Through how we speak, touch, decide, lead, and repair, we become participants in a universal wholeness that supports a future worthy of the next generation and those to come.

Above all, this book asks us to remember what we've always known: Life is relational, and its center is the heart we share.

Welcome to a path into the Communal Heart.

Part I

THE CRISIS OF MODERN CONNECTION

Chapter 1

WHEN ATTENTION SPLITS

We cannot solve our problems with the same
thinking we used when we created them.
—Albert Einstein

One of my favorite Saturday afternoon rituals used to be walking through the bright sunshine, then slipping into the cool shade beneath the tree-lined streets of the small college town where I live. I loved the scent of coffee drifting from the corner café, and the planters spilling over with color. Everyone would nod to say hello, some pausing for brief conversations, small gestures of recognition that gently stitched us together.

These days, however, the shared ease between people has shifted. Heads are down, shoulders are hunched, and eyes are glued to screens. People pass by one another without acknowledgment, their attention pulled inward. I can't help but feel a twinge of loneliness when I walk these streets now. It strikes me how common, how heartbreakingly familiar, this scene has become.

We've all had moments of standing in a crowded room and feeling alone. So, we turn to our phones for distraction, scrolling through hundreds of updates, yet still sense that nothing feels quite real or satisfying. Aching for more meaning, we look toward the future at a full calendar, wondering why, despite it all, we still feel empty.

These aren't passing moods. They're signals, faint stirrings from within and around us, that something essential is missing. Many of us are beginning to sense that this dissonance extends far beyond our personal lives, pointing to a fundamental imbalance woven into modern life. We may name it as burnout, polarization, or ecological collapse. But beneath these symptoms lies a story of disconnection. This chapter invites us to take a closer look at our growing sense of disconnection, trace these symptoms back to their source, and begin to recognize the larger pattern they reveal. What we uncover may not be easy to face, but it is the first step in healing the divide of modern life and moving toward reunion and greater wholeness.

The metacrisis we are living through is not simply a collection of separate crises to be solved in isolation but a single, interconnected rupture. It is the unraveling and fraying of the relational fabric that once held us together. To mend it, we must first understand how it came to be so torn apart.

LIFE IS RELATIONSHIP

Think about the last time you felt angry with someone. Maybe they showed up late to an important meeting, stepped on your toe without apologizing, or ate the last piece of cake you had been saving and looking forward to all day. Chances are that interaction stayed with you. It lingered until, in the presence of someone who cared, you were able to say what needed to be said and feel understood. This gesture began to set things right.

Relationships matter.

Even when we are alone, we are connected to the air we breathe, the food we eat, the sunlight on our skin, and the ache we carry in our hearts. We may not always feel it, but we live inside a web of mutuality. We affect our surroundings, and our surroundings, in turn, affect us. Life, with its consequences, doesn't merely move around us but moves through us. Yet the culture we live in tries to convince us of a different story.

Modern Western society conditions us to focus on what we do. We're measured by our output and defined by our accomplishments. Because agency is prized above all else, we tend to orient around what has been done to us or by us. As a result, we're encouraged to cultivate personal will, individual power, and self-determination, reinforcing an ethos of individualism that rewards status and fuels the addictive pull of success. Most of us know the drill: Hustle. Produce. Compete. Achieve.

However, with this elevation of agency comes its shadows. These unacknowledged burdens tend to manifest as feelings of shame, guilt, or resentment, depending on where we imagine ourselves to be on that scorecard of winners and losers. In an effort to cope with these weighty feelings, we develop the impulse to take rather than to receive. We begin to measure life by quantity instead of honoring the richness of quality. In the process, we not only strip the Earth of its resources but also learn to exploit one another emotionally, psychologically, and relationally. Gradually, we forget what it means to truly be with one another.

This model of one-way relating reduces others to objects to be managed rather than subjects to engage with. This pattern develops from a worldview based on separation, one that treats people as instruments, ecosystems as extractable resources, and time not as a space to inhabit but as a resource to conquer, optimize, and control. An extractive mindset shapes not only our social systems but also our inner lives. It is the cultural air we breathe.

Even healing spaces, such as therapy and coaching, are not immune. Increasingly, they are becoming tools of optimization, reinforcing the idea that we can bend life to our will. This is evident by the rise of social media influencers who capitalize on collective anxiety by offering branded solutions and expensive courses. Promises of empowerment and self-mastery are marketed in sleek packages, yet what is often sold is agency itself, a sense of personal power wrapped in certainty and offered up in uncertain times.

Of course, agency is important. It is a vital part of human development, after all. But agency alone isn't the whole story. In our modern pursuit of progress, we have lost touch with a far more fundamental way of meeting life. We have drifted from being. Being is as essential as doing. Being allows us to experience our surroundings without demanding they produce or prove anything to us. Being invites rest. Without moments to catch our breath, we grow weary and burn out. Being welcomes patience. Without the capacity to hold space, we rush ahead indiscriminately, and even our best intentions go astray. In other words, without a recognition of being, our attention toward doing becomes untethered, performative, and even hollow. We go through the motions, but the purpose drains out. We may appear engaged, but something crucial is missing. We lose the sense of alignment that tells us we are truly here, and that loss feels urgent.

Take modern healthcare, for example. How often do we worry about whether we can afford the medical care we need or whether we have access to it at all? How frequently do we feel unseen or unheard when our treatment is reduced to checklists or rushed physical exams? While these experiences may not happen all the time, they occur enough for us to feel like something is wrong. And it is not only patients who feel the strain.

The imbalance in attention is just as evident on the caregiving side. Medical professionals, overwhelmed by impossible workloads, are pressured to prioritize efficiency with little time to really connect with the people they serve. Healing becomes mechanical. Care, once grounded in relationship, loses its heart. The result is a system that leaves everyone, patients and medical providers alike, underserved and overextended.

Sadly, this pattern of time and connection imbalance is not confined to healthcare. It echoes across nearly every sector of modern society. In education, genuine learning is sacrificed for standardized metrics, and curiosity is stifled by the pressure to perform well on tests and grades. In politics, nuanced dialogue is replaced by sound bites, and ideological warfare drowns out any hope for collaboration. In our economies, human dignity is subordinated to productivity, and profit becomes the sole measure of success. Even in our most intimate relationships, the transactional mindset seeps in, reducing love to roles and emotional scorekeeping rather than allowing it to remain a living field of mutual respect and reciprocal care.

Beneath all of this runs a shared undercurrent of disconnection, a cultural forgetting of what it means to genuinely be in relationship—to listen, to empathize, and, above all, to be and belong.

THE BIAS TOWARD NARROW ATTENTION

A transactional way of reacting to the world has become so normalized that we rarely question it. We move at a pace that flattens complexity and overwhelms our nervous systems. We reach for quick fixes to deep-seated problems, and as a result, we lose touch not only with ourselves but also with one another and with the living world that sustains us. While we may feel disconnection emotionally in the form of anxiety or depression or interpret it intellectually as apathy or confusion, its roots are perceptual. The issue is not what we know but *how* we are relating to what we know—and what that way of attending makes possible.

Iain McGilchrist, a psychiatrist and philosopher, has written extensively about how our modern worldview has taken shape. According to his theory of the divided brain, our culture privileges a narrow, focused mode of attention, more characteristic of the left hemisphere. Although both hemispheres participate in meaning-making, a distinction we will explore later in the book, for now, it is helpful to understand that the left hemisphere primarily attends to what can be conceptually grasped and manipulated. It therefore favors abstraction, linearity, and analysis. When this mode of attention dominates, the world is increasingly approached as a collection of discrete parts, categorized and engaged instrumentally, and gradually detached from the wider relational and contextual field that gives those parts their meaning.[1]

For instance, within modern economic frameworks, nature is viewed largely as a set of resources to be extracted. Forests become "timber," rivers become "water supply," and human labor becomes "human capital." By abstracting life into measurable units, we gain efficiency but lose reverence for the living, interconnected world that makes life possible.

This same pattern shows up in our personal lives as well, when we objectify one another. We label people with "anxiety disorders," "avoidant attachments," or "narcissism," collapsing a human being into a fixed concept. What might otherwise be an opportunity for genuine contact and authentic connection instead becomes a narrowing of the relational space, shaped by power and control.

Yet this is only one way of perceiving. Its counterpart, the right hemisphere, is different but complementary. It tends to open toward broad, contextual awareness, attuning to patterns and to how parts belong within a living whole. When this mode of attention is predominant, it is grounded in direct, embodied experience and supports a more relational, rather than instrumental, way of attending.[2] When we engage in broader attention, rather than simply labeling someone, we begin to see a human being managing their energy in relation to each context: an anxious person as someone who has lost internal or external support; an avoidant person as someone who has withdrawn to conserve energy; or a narcissistic person as someone who has walled themselves off to protect against further perceived harm. As these fixed categories soften, the complexity of the relationship opens into a meeting with what is alive and real between us.

Unfortunately, modern life has tilted too far in one direction, toward favoring narrow attention. If the brain is a symphony, the right hemisphere is the conductor, and the left is the first violin. We have handed the baton to the violinist and asked him to lead the entire orchestra. The result is an orchestra, our modern culture, playing out of tune and out of rhythm with life itself.

You may feel this dissonance when you become fixated on trying to solve a problem, perhaps between you and another person, and a sense of vitality begins to disappear. You attend closely to the details, refining and adjusting to get them right. However, the more you focus, the more the larger context falls from view. What you're doing may seem coherent on its own, but the life has gone out of it.

This is what happens when attention has narrowed so completely that the wider field is lost. Without the right hemisphere's ability to hold context, meaning fragments. Nuance, emotion, and relational depth fade, and what remains is technically accurate but strangely flat. In trying to fix the problem, we inadvertently sever the very thread that connects us and brings us into harmony with a whole.

While our inner fragmentation becomes mirrored in the world around us, our cultural predicament won't be solved by doubling down on the very patterns that created it. What we need instead is to cultivate balanced attention, not just widening what we pay attention to but changing how we relate to what we perceive. As we begin to attend to the whole, our perception shifts. We recognize that we are not isolated individuals but intricately interwoven beings. Relationship is not peripheral to life. *It is life.* It must be remembered, nurtured, and restored.

This relational work begins by reconnecting to our own being through the cultivation of presence. Unlike mindfulness as it is usually practiced today, the presence we will cultivate in this book is more than a technique. It is a way of meeting the world. Based on Gestalt Practice, it involves developing embodied awareness by directing attention to our sensations, emotions, surroundings, and the mental patterns and narratives through which we make meaning.

When doing and being come into balance through presence, we remember our relatedness—the felt sense that we are always in relationship with ourselves, each other, the Earth, and the larger systems that shape us and are shaped by us. As we begin to feel into this existential truth, we soften and then open. We begin to honor what is easily overlooked: The quality of our connections is as important as, if not more than, the number of connections we make. When we value how we show up for one another, a different kind of intelligence begins to emerge, not simply cognitive intelligence but relational intelligence. Relational intelligence is the wisdom we seek when we feel distance between ourselves and the world around us, for it is the capacity to hold, attune, respond, and integrate that closes this gap.

When presence begins to settle within us, we reach outward and start to embrace mutuality, and a bidirectional flow of presence starts to move between us, nourishing us and carrying us further than we could ever go on our own. From there, we are invited to cultivate coherence, the integrity that arises when our inner and outer worlds align with a shared purpose among us.

Fortunately, the guidance we need to begin this restoration is not far away. It lives within our bodies, embedded in the fabric of relationships, waiting patiently to be remembered. As we continue down this path into the Communal Heart, we will explore various qualities of relational intelligence with more intention and depth—specifically, presence, mutuality, and coherence.

THE APPRECIATION OF DIFFERENCE

One of the most frequent complaints I hear from new mothers in my psychotherapy practice is their surprise, and often frustration, that their partners, usually a husband or boyfriend, can sleep through the sound of a crying baby at night. Likewise, many women share that they seem to carry the emotional pulse of the household, while the men in their lives appear more concerned with practical things.

Of course, these role divisions are not universal or fixed. More and more men are stepping into primary caregiving roles, staying home with young children as their partners pursue professions outside the home. Yet even in these more progressive arrangements, many working mothers still report holding the bulk of the relational labor. They tend not only to their children's needs but also to the emotional dynamics of extended family, friendships, and professional relationships, all while wondering out loud whether the fathers of their children even care.

When I press further, however, a more nuanced picture emerges. These men do care, and they attempt to show it by focusing on different domains, such as maintaining physical systems of the home and managing household risk. So, the problem isn't always a lack of concern; it's a difference in what is being noticed, prioritized, and then acted upon.

While contemporary neuroscience has not found reliable evidence that men and women differ in hemispheric dominance or in the fundamental attentional and perceptual modes described in McGilchrist's divided-brain theory, behavioral research does suggest consistent group-level differences in what men and women tend to find most salient or engaging. On average, men are more likely to orient attention toward how things work, while women are more often attuned to how people relate.[3] These general patterns are neither random nor purely socially constructed, even as culture influences how they are expressed. When viewed through an evolutionary lens, they begin to make sense.

Because human infants are born exceptionally dependent, early caregiving contexts placed a premium on heightened sensitivity to emotional and nonverbal cues. Survival in these conditions depended on the caregiver's capacity for attunement—the ability to notice, feel into, and respond sensitively to an infant's internal state through sustained presence. This form of relational intelligence precedes language and plays a central role in supporting physiological regulation and the development of secure attachment.

At the same time, early caregiving placed mothers and infants in conditions of profound vulnerability and exposure. Across many small-scale societies, with considerable variation across ecologies, this vulnerability was buffered through complementary divisions of labor, often including males in provisioning and protection from external threats. These roles favored a more goal-directed mode of attention, one that organizes perception around outcomes, making instrumental agency not only possible but often primary, in service of the safety of kin and community.

Together, these complementary modes of attention form a dynamic polarity that appears repeatedly in human social life: one oriented toward relational presence, the other to instrumental agency. While historically emphasized differently in women and men, they are neither fixed traits nor exclusive. Rather, they are shared human capacities whose integration has been essential to the survival and flourishing of early human groups.[4]

Although these attentional tendencies remain necessary for human coherence, modern Western culture has, over time, increasingly privileged one mode of attention over the other, favoring mechanistic objectification over relational attunement. Our collective attention has tilted toward how things work, while the art of how we get along has faded into the background. To point out this imbalance is not a critique of men, per se, but an honest acknowledgment of how biology, history, and cultural design have configured the architecture of modern life. For millennia, public domains such as governance, economics, and science were structured almost exclusively by male participation. In the United States, for example, it has been just over a century since women were granted the right to vote and participate formally in public discourse.[5] Because most of our modern systems were built predominantly by men and shaped by a mode of attention oriented toward instrumental agency, we have been culturally trained to analyze and then construct. However, this emphasis frequently comes at the expense of staying connected to the broader field of meaning that arises through relationship, emotional nuance, and contextual awareness. The result is a world brimming with tools yet starving for tenderness.[6]

Given this history, it is no surprise that many of our dominant institutional structures are shaped by a narrow, goal-directed mode of attention—one that has undeniably fueled extraordinary advances in science, technology, and governance. Yet in the process, other vital ways of knowing have been sidelined, particularly the relational, contextual, and life-affirming capacities that likely evolved under caregiving pressures and are therefore often associated with the feminine. These capacities arise from a broader, more receptive mode of awareness, one attuned not only to outcomes, but to the web of relationships that sustain life.

The deeper issue, for this book and for our culture, is not whether the masculine and feminine tendencies neatly map onto left- and right-hemispheric modes of attention, nor whether mechanistic and relational orientations appear more often in men and women. Those questions are important, but they are not the most pressing ones. What's at stake is what begins to unravel when these capacities fall out of balance, regardless of who carries them. When abstraction is consistently elevated above relationship, and agency valued over attunement, we lose touch with the very qualities that make connection and meaning possible. Presence fades. Responsiveness gives way to efficiency alone. And we forget that these relational capacities are not luxuries but essential conditions for sustaining life—individually, collectively, and culturally.[7]

THE CALL OF THE COMMUNAL HEART

The good news is that we are not bound by these inherited patterns. As human beings, we carry an innate capacity to interrupt them, to choose differently, and to begin again. By bringing into awareness what was once unconscious, we can begin to integrate our different ways of perceiving into a more coherent and animating whole, first within ourselves and then within the systems we co-create. In other words, we can learn to broaden our attention to include the whole field: to listen not only to what is spoken but to the way meaning speaks through us. By attuning to what is felt, intuited, and sensed beneath the surface, we begin to relate not merely through roles or functions but through presence. To be, not just to do.

Many of us have had a taste of this when we needed it most. After a long, difficult day, we come home, drop our bags, and sink into a chair with a heavy sigh. A friend or partner walks in, not with advice or solutions, but sits beside us. With their balanced attention fully on us, they convey, "I'm here with you." They don't try to solve anything. Perhaps they offer a warm drink or place a gentle hand on our back. In their steady presence, we begin to let go. We feel seen, not for how well we've coped or how strong we've been, but simply for being human—tired, tender, and trying.

No problem has been solved, but the weight begins to lift. We are no longer alone with our heartache. Moments like these remind us that a deeper and more sustaining way of meeting the world is possible. This is the heart of restoring relational intelligence in our personal lives and across every layer of our culture. By honoring the generative tension between the impulse to assert and the capacity to hold, we bring these two ways of relating into conscious balance. From that balance, a new possibility emerges, not merely more efficient systems but a wiser and more compassionate society.[8]

If the metacrisis we face reflects a rupture in relationship, then the path into the Communal Heart offers a profoundly human response. By broadening our attention, we remember what was never truly lost and return to the relational field that makes healing and wholeness possible.

In Chapter 2, we will explore how the costs of disconnection manifest in our bodies, relationships, and felt sense of belonging in the natural world. Mending the world does not begin with fixing. It begins by becoming intimately acquainted with the fragmentations within, between, and among us.

Chapter 2
WHERE WE COME PULLED APART

When we try to pick out anything by itself, we find it hitched to everything else in the universe.
—John Muir

I have had clients describe it like this: "It's not that anything is terribly wrong. It's that nothing feels fully right." Some of us feel this unnerving quality in the tightening of our shoulders as we open our inboxes in the morning, already bracing for what is to come. For others, it appears as a low-grade anxiety humming just beneath the surface of awareness, even in the tranquil moments right before sunset. Still others experience it as a deep, almost unnamable weariness that settles into our bones as we lie awake at night, trying to rest.

A relational fracture is not just a concept; it is a lived experience, one that takes up residence in the body, heart, and soul.

Although we are more digitally connected than ever before, our inner lives and our relationships with others tell a different story. This state of unrest goes beyond ordinary stress or personal overwhelm. It reflects the psychological toll of living within systems that no longer honor our natural state of being. We're wired for embodied awareness and mutual recognition, but we've built lives, usually out of necessity, within social structures that reward speed over emotional depth and performance over relational connection. And we're paying a hefty price for this way of living.

According to the World Health Organization, depression is now the leading cause of disability worldwide.[1] When we lose connection to our own needs and emotions, we become estranged from the very sources of vitality that sustain us. This personal disconnection reflects a broader cultural narrative. In societies that prize achievement over well-being, our worth becomes tethered to what we produce rather than who we are. We start to see ourselves as interchangeable parts in an impersonal, mechanistic system. But our decline in mental health points less to individual failures. Instead, it is a sign of a more profound fragmentation, indicating that the ways we live are out of step with what makes us most human.

THE FRAGMENTATION WITHIN US

Disconnection begins in the most intimate of places: within ourselves.

Because we live in a culture that rewards productivity, we frequently lose touch with ourselves in our perpetual rush to keep up.

We bypass the simple act of slowing down to breathe. We neglect to register how we feel. And we tune out the voices within that speak not in metrics or deadlines but in resonance with what gives life meaning and direction.

I once worked with a mid-career professional, wife, and mother, Samira, who had always seen herself as highly efficient. She juggled multiple projects, managed a team, stayed active on social media, and kept up with her social obligations. From the outside, she appeared to be thriving, but inside, she felt empty, as if she were running on autopilot.

Her mornings began with a rapid scroll through her phone, checking notifications before even getting out of bed. Meetings filled her day, leaving little time to reflect. When she finally got home, she usually felt too drained to engage meaningfully with her family. Instead, she would numb out with videos or late-night doomscrolling. Over time, an unshakeable emptiness surfaced that she couldn't quite name.

One evening, Samira sat down for dinner with her ten-year-old son, Cyrus. As he excitedly shared a school project, she instinctively reached for her phone. He paused mid-sentence and sighed, "Never mind, Mom. You're too busy." While she'd heard those words before, this time, they landed differently. A quiet recognition broke through the fog: "I'm so sorry, Cyrus," she said softly. "You're right. I'm distracted. I'm going to put my phone away, and then I want to hear all about your day." In that instant, she realized how far she had drifted, not only from her son, but from herself as well. Samira had mistaken constant productivity for meaning and efficiency for being present. In her pursuit of external success, she had lost her ability to fully be with herself and those she loved.

Samira's experience is far from unique. In a culture that prioritizes doing over being, many of us have become disconnected from our own inner worlds. Eventually, this fragmentation begins to erode our mental and emotional well-being, as well as our capacity to relate to ourselves, to those we love, and to the deeper current of meaning that makes life truly worth living. The result is that our lives may appear full from the outside, with busy schedules and even measurable success, but inside, many of us feel hollow.

THE FRAGMENTATION BETWEEN US

Unfortunately, what begins as disconnection within ourselves inevitably reverberates outward. When we lose touch with our inner life, our capacity to relate meaningfully with others begins to fray, too. A few years ago, a client named Lin described sitting in her car outside her own home, unable to go inside. She saw her toddler crying through the window, while her wife was on the couch next to their son, unobservant, scrolling on her phone. Lin wasn't angry exactly, simply numb. "I'm surrounded by people I love," she said, "but I feel like I'm disappearing." What she named in that moment wasn't necessarily exhaustion. It was the ache of disconnection, the slow erosion of no longer feeling seen, supported, and known.

As the texture of relationships shifts, we go through the motions but feel the absence of closeness and depth. Misunderstandings begin to increase. Emotional labor becomes uneven. Conversations skim the surface or become reactive. In turn, our communities wane, not because we don't care but because we're too distracted or overwhelmed to show up in the ways we long to.

Public discourse bears the marks of this disconnection, too. It fractures under the weight of outrage and the compulsive performance of certainty. We stop approaching one another with curiosity or generosity. Instead, we categorize, defend, and eventually withdraw because we no longer trust that we can bring ourselves forward in any constructive and meaningful way. Conversations collapse into persuasion or posturing, and the relational field, once alive with the possibility of mutual understanding, grows brittle and tense. As many of us well know, trust erodes, not only in individuals but also in our institutions and the leaders we are supposed to rely on.

In short, this fragmentation is not only emotional or psychological; it is also structural.

Erosion of social connection is most evident in the disappearance of communal spaces. A comprehensive 2026 survey by Rocket Mortgage found that fewer than 30 percent of Americans report feeling a strong connection to their neighbors.[2] Neighborhoods that once invited gathering now sprawl in ways that isolate. Streets are built for speed and traffic rather than for impromptu get-togethers with neighbors and pickup basketball games. Digital screens replace shared experience. And the commons—the porches, parks, plazas, and public spaces where people once naturally encountered one another—are vanishing or are rendered inhospitable. Perhaps the starkest symptom of this shift is how many of us now live near people we barely know, struggling in private while surrounded by others doing the same. Each of us quietly believes our loneliness is a personal failing, rather than recognizing it as a collective wound.

We are made for connection. Yet the very systems we've built pull us further apart. Until we begin to name and actually feel the cost of that separation, we remain caught in a cycle that diminishes our humanity and weakens the bonds that hold us together.

THE FRAGMENTATION BEYOND US

Beyond our personal and interpersonal lives, perhaps the most visible and urgent fracture of all is the rift between humanity and the natural world. For centuries, dominant cultural narratives have framed humans as separate from and superior to nature, leading to exploitative relationships with the Earth. This mindset has contributed to climate change, driving what scientists now refer to as the sixth mass extinction. Current extinction rates are estimated to be one hundred to one thousand times higher than natural background rates and are accelerating.[3]

The ecological consequences of domination over nature are staggering. Human activities have already caused approximately 1.1°C of global warming above pre-industrial levels, devastating ecosystems and disproportionately affecting vulnerable communities.[4] A fragmented mindset is symptomatic of a broken relationship with our most significant source of support. These symptoms show us what happens when we lose our felt sense of belonging to the natural world. When that connection breaks, so too do the feedback loops that sustain life. We forget that we are not separate from nature. We are nature, shaped by its intelligence, participating in its rhythms, and bound to its fate.

This disconnection is not merely ecological, but also profoundly spiritual. The forest no longer speaks to us. The river is no longer regarded as kin. The wind no longer carries messages we are taught to hear. In that silence, life-sustaining intuition begins to wither. Without a relationship with the Earth, reverence becomes rare. Without reverence, care becomes unsustainable.

These inner, social, and ecological fragmentations are not isolated. They interlock and reinforce one another, forming a self-perpetuating system of disconnection that infiltrates every dimension of our lives. When we are cut off from our inner experience, we are more likely to engage in ways that perpetuate disconnection in our relationships and communities. After all, fragmented individuals give rise to fragmented cultures, and those cultures, in turn, create systems that mirror and intensify disconnection. These systems gradually weaken our innate bonds with the Earth. Over time, the feedback loop tightens, making disconnection feel not only familiar but inevitable too.

We see this phenomenon reflected in our institutions. Our criminal justice system usually prioritizes punishment over restoration.[5] Schools tend to prize standardization over honoring the uniqueness of each child.[6] And our cities are largely designed for efficiency, not for human connection.[7] We have built external structures that reflect our internal fragmentation—social environments that feel increasingly alien, even to those who created them.

And then we wonder why we do not feel at home.

RETURNING TO THE RELATIONAL FIELD

But this predicament need not be the end of the story. The very fact that we feel the pain of disconnection reveals that we still carry the memory of wholeness within us. It lives in our bodies, just beneath the surface of daily life. It rises in mindful moments of stillness, in the presence of genuine care, in encounters with real beauty, and in the unmistakable feeling of belonging. These moments remind us that we are not meant to live fragmented lives.

To begin reweaving the fabric of modern life, we must reclaim our attention, turning it inward, outward, among us, and even beyond. This means becoming aware of our breath, sensing the emotional tone beneath a conversation, and recognizing the subtle intelligence that pulses through the more-than-human world. Activating our relational intelligence in this manner develops our capacity to feel, attune, and respond in ways that honor the integrity of the whole. This is not a sentimental ideal. It is an essential skill for a world on the brink. And it asks something remarkable of us.

It calls for integration.

We are being asked to bring together what modern society has long held apart. Broad, contextual awareness, attuned to nuance and relational depth, finds its fullest expression when held in partnership with focused discernment, oriented toward abstraction and instrumental action. These different ways of knowing and attending are not binaries to be collapsed, but complementary intelligences and relational capacities held in creative tension.

When brought into balance, they do not cancel one another out. Instead, they co-create a relational field in which something new can emerge, something wise enough to perceive the whole and strong enough to serve it.

To access this wholeness, we must first reckon with what keeps us fragmented in the first place. Disconnection not only affects our well-being, but also distorts how we see and make sense of the world. When we are fractured within, we begin to confuse control with safety, productivity with worth, and isolation with independence. These distortions become so normalized that we hardly notice them, yet they quietly shape our choices, our relationships, and our sense of what is possible.

In Chapter 3, we explore the path of return, not as a retreat into an idealized past but as a reweaving of what has been torn. This return allows us to meet the complexity of our time with greater coherence and an expanded capacity for collective action. Through the practice of presence, we begin to reclaim our sense of belonging and reconnect with what has been forgotten. We remember how to listen from the inside out. When we do, we reclaim what our culture has rendered elusive but remains essential: the experience of wholeness that arises through the integration of these complementary ways of knowing and attending.

Chapter 3

HOW WE FIND OUR WAY HOME

Wherever you are is the entry point.
—Kabir

Have you ever walked into a room and forgotten why you entered? You pause, retrace your steps, and maybe even laugh at yourself. However, sometimes, it is more than a temporary lapse. It is a feeling that lingers. You feel you've lost touch with something vital, not just in the room, but in your life as well. Many of us are living this way. We move quickly, accomplish much, yet quietly wonder why we still feel incomplete, so far from ourselves and from what we value most.

Wholeness is not achieved by fixing ourselves. Wholeness is remembered by returning to who we already are. Beneath the frenzy of striving and the debris of disconnection lies a deeper current of awareness: We are part of a living field, shaped and sustained by relationships. This relational field is the Communal Heart.

Most of us have been taught to override this existential truth. We've learned to mistrust our bodies, to downplay our emotions, and to confine knowing to the mind alone. We push through, numb out, and perform instead of embody. Finding our way back home to ourselves and the world to which we belong begins with cultivating embodied awareness, or presence, as a grounding relational practice. Presence invites us to re-inhabit our bodies, slow down enough to feel again, and listen for the finely layered intelligence that speaks through sensation, rhythm, and breath.

A SUBTLE RHYTHM

Because modern life teaches us to rely almost entirely on our minds, we are infatuated by its linearity and analytic precision. The intellectual intelligence of the mind has enabled the creation of complex systems, the calculation of risks, and the solution of difficult problems. Minds have mapped the stars and created unbelievable technologies that save lives. Although in becoming dominant, linear thinking also distances us from the more subtle and equally vital intelligence of the heart.

Relational intelligence operates differently. Rather than analyzing, it attunes. Instead of grasping for control, it responds with care. It does not impose its will. On the contrary, relational intelligence listens deeply and moves to a gentler beat. This form of knowing lives in our bodies, in the tone of our voices, and in the quality of awareness we bring to ourselves and each other.

When we begin to return to this subtle, natural rhythm, we settle down. We stop rushing past our own lives and start to inhabit them more fully. In response, we remember what truly matters, not as an abstract idea or another task to complete, but as an embodied experience. This shift in awareness marks a return to a more integrated way of being. *It is a way home.*

I once worked with Shoshanna, a high-achieving executive in the tech industry. She was sharp, efficient, and endlessly productive. Her decisiveness had earned her admiration and propelled her upward. Even so, beneath that polished surface, she was falling apart. She was exhausted. She shared that her relationships were strained. The joy she once felt in her work had dulled. Her body, tired of being ignored, had begun to speak through illness and fatigue.

One day, during a standard work meeting, the unexpected happened. Her favorite and most successful employee approached her, voice shaking, and said, "I think I am going to find another placement." Then she went on, "We're so focused on efficiency here that we've forgotten how to care for our work, let alone one another."

Shoshanna cracked open. In that rupture, she saw, for the first time, the actual cost of her success—the toll it had taken on her own well-being as well as on the people around her. She began to realize that her team didn't need more performance metrics, tighter deadlines, or firmer control. What they needed was far more human. They needed the acknowledgment that behind every role was a person doing the best they could with what they had. In that exchange, Shoshanna realized that leadership is not only about holding everything together, but also about creating the conditions where people can show up more fully as who they really are.

To her credit, Shoshanna began to shift. She created space for regular employee-focused check-ins. She invited candor into the room. She stopped treating relational dynamics as peripheral distractions and began to recognize them as central to the work. The impact went beyond the emotional. It was tangible. As trust grew, turnover decreased and creativity returned. The atmosphere became warmer and more human. What emerged was not just a healthier team, but a more coherent one, grounded in mutual respect and shared purpose.

Shoshanna's story may seem improbable in a world that frequently rewards success over human dignity, but it is critical. Recognizing the innate dignity in others reminds us of the felt sense of coherence, embodied and mutual. When we bring relational intelligence to one another and to the relational field that we shape and are shaped by, we shift. We attune to reality as it is rather than as we imagine it to be. When we abide by reality's subtle rhythm, we can begin to serve life. In this space, we are no longer reduced to functional roles or outputs. We are honored as whole human beings. And dignity, so often an afterthought, becomes the very ground from which meaningful progress can emerge.

EMBODYING RELATIONALITY

Coherence is not only an idea to grasp, but also a reality to live into. The natural, rhythmic movement from fragmentation into wholeness is a fundamentally sentient process that begins in sensation and breath, reminding us we are here. It is the reawakening of our embodied sense of belonging—what many of us have forgotten but, fortunately, never truly lost. It lives in the pulse beneath our skin, in the way we soften when met with care, and in the feeling of aliveness that arises when we stop bracing against life.

Perhaps you've experienced it before, a fleeting but vivid moment when everything seemed exactly right. Maybe it was with your child, a dear friend, or in a place that felt comforting, when life didn't need to be improved or explained, only received. Your senses came alive in the way the light fell just so, the sound of the cat's purring, or the scent of dinner on the stove or rain on warm pavement. It is the opposite of entering a room and not remembering your purpose for being there. You weren't rushing through or reaching for more. You were simply present. I imagine you relaxed, opened, and responded. Gratitude may have arisen, unforced. In that moment, you weren't merely observing life. You were in it. Anchored. Alive. Aware that you were part of something larger than yourself.

These experiences offer a glimpse of what it means to return to our relatedness, a return that begins by embodying awareness. As awareness is grounded in lived experience, presence naturally emerges. By cultivating presence, we learn to reconnect with ourselves, with one another, and with what is most essential: our participation in the field of awareness as a relational, embodied reality. This is what lies at the center of the Communal Heart.

CULTIVATING RELATIONAL CAPACITIES IS A PATH

Because the path into the Communal Heart outlined in this book is rooted in relationality, it unfolds through the cultivation of five primary relational capacities: presence, mutuality, coherence, attunement, and integration. Presence invites us to meet life as it is, grounding awareness in the immediacy of experience. Mutuality grows from that ground, reminding us that a relationship is a living exchange between self and other, rather than a one-way act. Coherence arises as these connections align, bringing the harmony we have cultivated within ourselves into resonance with the world around us, so that what we think, feel, and do moves as one. The first three capacities develop through attunement, a responsiveness to the subtle rhythms within and around us, and are gathered into more complete wholeness through integration. Together, all five capacities form a dynamic, cyclical dance of relational becoming that restores wholeness within, between, and among us. Let's take a closer look at this path.

Presence (Attuning Within)

Reconnection begins within, and cultivating presence is the first step. By broadening our attention to include body, breath, heartbeat, and sensations, we anchor ourselves to the here and now.

Presence, or embodied awareness, is not passive. It is a form of active receptivity that invites us to slow down, notice, and choose how we meet each moment, rather than simply react out of fear, habit, or performance. In a world driven by productivity and status, turning toward the quiet undertones of lived reality that presence illuminates slows the pace of overwhelm, restores balance, and returns us to the ground of shared belonging.

This quality of attentional availability opens the doorway to careful listening. As we slow down enough to feel our inner states, we reclaim the capacity to respond to the steady stream of sensory input with intention. From this grounded awareness, we can engage life's complexity with greater coherence, more attuned to what each moment is truly asking of us.

Presence in this context is not a spiritual ideal so much as a necessity. It is the foundation upon which all other relational capacities are built. Without it, the human-environmental connection remains shallow. With it, we begin to sense the deeper rhythm of life and relationship.

Take, for example, the situation in which you are about to give a presentation at work. Your heart is racing, your palms are sweaty, and your mind is spinning with what-ifs. You feel the urge to push past the discomfort and "power through," but you pause instead. You take a slow breath, feel your feet on the floor, the weight of your body in the chair, and the rise and fall of your chest. You notice your anxiety and acknowledge it. You place a hand on your belly and let your exhale become longer. Slowly, your nervous system begins to settle. You are not trying to be somewhere else. You are here.

That is embodiment.

To be embodied is not about achieving perfect calm or eliminating fear. It means fully inhabiting your experience and allowing awareness to drop from the linear activity of the mind into the natural responsiveness of the body. When you act through embodied awareness, words and actions arise not only from your mind, but also from a grounded, felt sense of presence—and others can feel the difference.

Mutuality (Attuning Between)

From presence, we naturally move outward to restore our connection with others. Mutuality is the practice of shared, reciprocal engagement, meeting others with humility, navigating differences with care, and attending to the essential work of repairing ruptures when feelings get hurt. Mutuality invites us to show up openhearted in our relationships, even when it feels difficult.

In mutuality, fairness and care become values that guide our interactions. Rather than a static formula, mutuality is a social commitment to the well-being of all. Here, we begin to feel our interdependence and experience the courage it takes to be in sincere relationship with one another, especially when the path is not easy.

Imagine you're sitting at a subway station when an elderly woman walks up, luggage in hand. Even though your back aches from having moved furniture the day before, you stand and offer her your seat. She accepts with a warm nod. As you both wait, the silence gives way to conversation. Her tone is kind, and her curiosity is genuine.

As the conversation continues, she happens to mention your neighborhood and then your son. Your mind flashes to a recent frustration. Your son had shared that this very neighbor had complained about him being too loud while skateboarding in the street. You brace for a repeat of that complaint, but the exchange takes an unexpected turn.

The elderly woman speaks of how lonely the past few years have been since her husband died. She remembers how she used to enjoy hearing the sounds of communal life—her husband playing the guitar and birdsongs drifting through open windows. But lately, the silence in her own home has grown heavy. She admits, a bit sheepishly, that the complaint wasn't really about the noise: "I feel like I don't even belong in my own neighborhood anymore."

In that instant, your defenses go down. You see past the behavior and into the need beneath it. What started as an act of courtesy becomes a doorway to understanding. A bridge forms not only between two people, but also between generations, personal stories, and unspoken feelings. You make a mental note to tell your son to perhaps reframe how he sees this neighbor, not as a grumpy woman, but as someone who, like all of us, just wants to belong without knowing how.

Coherence (Attuning Among)

As mutuality grows, coherence begins to emerge. Coherence is a felt alignment between our inner truth, the presence of others, and the outer relational field that shapes our lives. It is not sameness but a dignified unity that arises when diverse perspectives and intentions begin to align in service of something greater than any one individual or the sum of individual perspectives or concerns combined. Coherence helps us see how our personal patterns are intertwined with broader social, ecological, and ancestral dynamics. It supports us in living with intention and a sense of shared purpose.

Can you recall a time when you were part of a group—perhaps playing music, dancing, or even playing a team sport—and a subtle but profound shift began to occur? A sense of effortless flow emerged, when you felt fully yourself while also deeply connected to others. The boundaries between "you" and "them" likely blurred. Words became unnecessary, and a shared rhythm took hold. You weren't just participating; you were part of a larger unity, guided not by individual control but by tacit harmony generated by and through the group. This is coherence. It is an experience that arises when presence and mutuality converge, allowing a shared current of meaning to move through you and those around you.

Attunement (Resonating With)

Attunement can be thought of as the relational "glue" that restores this kind of connection, because it is the way through which we resonate with ourselves, others, and the non-human world. It enables the shift from mere awareness to recognizing that we have the ability and, more importantly, the responsibility to choose consciously and act from that choice. This requires trusting our capacity to respond to the situation we find ourselves in by orienting our awareness "skin-side in" to our inner sensations and feelings, "skin-side out" to our surroundings, and "in between" to our thoughts and interpretations. In essence, attunement is a quality of attention that listens beyond words, senses what is felt and intuited, and notices what is moving beneath the surface of our immediate reactions.

The following examples illustrate how attunement moves us along the path of restoring connection within, between, and among us.

Self-attuning toward presence: You are about to send a frustrated email. Your chest feels tight, your jaw is clenched, and your thoughts are racing. You pause. You take a breath. You feel the tension in your body and recognize that underneath your anger is hurt, maybe even sadness. Instead of hitting "Send," you sit with the discomfort for a few more breaths, allowing yourself to feel what is actually there. You realize you need connection, not conflict, and begin reconsidering the stance of your email. This shift from reactivity to presence is self-attunement arising from awareness. It is a moment of noticing, choosing, and then responding from a place of aligning one's needs with the circumstances from which they emerge.

Relational attuning toward mutuality: A boy falls and scrapes his knee. He's trying to suppress his cry. His mother kneels, makes eye contact, and says gently, "That looked like it hurt," signaling to her son that she is there with and for him. At the same time, the mother does not rush to put a bandage over the wound or minimize her son's pain. Instead, she meets him emotionally, mirroring his experience with warmth and steadiness. This external support allows the boy to relax into his own experience and respond according to his bodily needs. Slowly, he begins to cry, releasing what was held inside to make room for his eventual healing, while his mother feels reassured, knowing her presence has given him the safety to let go and begin to reclaim himself. Relational attunement involves being with someone, not just physically, but emotionally in sync with their inner world as well, and then responding to what the situation requires, no more and no less.

Group attuning toward coherence: Imagine a team of healthcare workers in the emergency department during a crisis. Tensions are high, decisions need to be made quickly, and everyone is under pressure. A physician notices that the team is beginning to fragment. Communication is rushed, some team members are shutting down, and small mistakes are creeping in. Instead of pushing harder or ignoring the signs, the doctor slows down to ground herself, makes eye contact with the lead nurse, and calmly says, "Let's take a breath and check in for a few seconds." The team pauses, and a collective breath is taken. People reconnect. Their eyes meet, and their body language softens. The head nurse gently checks in with the newest staff member to let them know what is about to happen next. As a result, the energy shifts from reactive to responsive. From that point on, the medical team moves with greater clarity and rhythm. Communication becomes more fluid and effective, and responsibilities are more naturally shared. Each person remains focused but also aware of the group as a whole. No one is working in isolation, nor is anyone being micromanaged. This is group attunement, where individuals tune into both themselves and one another, enabling coherence to arise through coordinated action in service of a shared purpose.

Integration (Restoring Wholeness)

Integration is the process of bringing all these relational capacities within ourselves, between people, or across larger systems into relationship, so they can move together in a harmonious and life-giving way. Let's take a closer look at how integration takes shape across different realms of our lives.

Returning to inner wholeness: Within oneself, integration involves aligning thoughts, emotions, bodily sensations, and actions so that our inner experience becomes less fragmented and more coherent. This work involves acknowledging and including previously suppressed or conflicting capacities of the self. Aligning our inner experience restores broad, contextual awareness to its rightful place alongside narrow, focused attention so that we can perceive more clearly, choose more wisely, and respond more appropriately to the situations we find ourselves in. For example, when we are integrated, we feel more at home in our own skin and can more easily access our inner resources, responding with confidence to the circumstances we are in. We are more able to identify what we need, communicate it clearly, and find support, both within ourselves and in the world around us, for the challenges we face. However, integration does not imply being entirely in control or constantly composed. It reflects our capacity to trust ourselves to respond appropriately to the situations we encounter.

Restoring mutual regard: Between people, integration manifests as an honest, mutual recognition where commonalities are acknowledged and differences are respected so that social trust can grow between us. It consists of communication and action that support both our independence and our interdependence. It calls us to appreciate our innate perceptual orientations, whether they lean toward a receptive, contextual mode or a direct, focused mode, while recognizing our capacity to move fluidly between them. Integration begins when we listen deeply to one another, encouraging what is more alive in the other to awaken within ourselves. Through this process, we learn to value not only what is being said, but also how it is being expressed—the energetic quality beneath the words that invites growth and balance. For example, a couple learning to integrate their relational capacities speaks openly about the deeper layers of their experience. They understand how their family histories, formative wounds, and personal values shape their reactions. Rather than simply defending themselves, they share the background from which behaviors arise. This self-disclosure creates space for greater empathy, helping their partner not only understand what they do but also why it is important to them. In this way, integration invites relational intimacy by allowing each person to be more fully seen, known, and met.

Healing the collective field: Among a group or systems, integration fosters cultures that honor diverse perspectives. When multiple ways of seeing are valued, collective intelligence can emerge, supporting communal coordination toward a shared purpose without fragmentation or collapse. Valuing perspective requires honoring feminine ways of knowing alongside masculine ones, especially in modern societies where the latter have long dominated governance structures, institutions, and models of leadership. Integration among groups and systems balances fairness and care, ensuring that discernment is guided by compassion and that decision-making is rooted not only in logic and efficiency but also in embodied awareness and relational wisdom. For example, rather than focusing solely on outcomes, an integrated system or institution also values the well-being of all those involved in bringing those outcomes to bear. Sustainable success is understood to arise not from extraction, but from honoring the people who make the work possible. In such systems, care and coherence are woven into the very structure, ensuring that both purpose and people are held with equal importance.

Each of these examples shows how attunement naturally leads to integration, allowing what was once separate to come back into relationship with the context that gave rise to it. Integration, in this sense, is like the slow, mindful closing of a zipper: Each tooth that was apart finds its corresponding match until a coherent whole is restored. Yet integration is not a final destination but an ongoing rhythm, a continual return to wholeness that deepens with every cycle. By holding the dynamic interplay of presence, mutuality, and coherence, integration gathers what has been scattered and, through attunement, invites it back into a living, continuous process of belonging.

Most importantly, integration enables us to hold paradoxes, like agency and surrender, difference and unity, and stillness and movement. It unites the inner and outer with the personal and the collective, creating space for what was once fragmented to coalesce in a new, generative way. In doing so, it reconnects us to our full humanity, helping us remember the wisdom of our becoming participants in an ever-changing, evolving world.

A RETURN TO BELONGING

Clearly, the journey toward wholeness is not a solitary act. Though it begins in the body through embodied awareness, it radiates outward, shaping how we meet one another, how we respond to life, and how we allow ourselves to be touched by the world around us. This is a path into the Communal Heart, and it is one we walk now together through the remainder of this book.

In the chapters ahead, we will explore how this path unfolds, from cultivating presence and healing our relationships to imagining new cultural possibilities and integrating growth within and among us. As we reenter the field of belonging, we begin to sense life's rhythms—those that cannot be forced, only met. Part II opens with an attunement to these natural rhythms that invite our deeper participation. By tuning into life's cycles, we rediscover a sacred cadence that both orients us and draws us home.

Part II

RETURNING TO OURSELVES

Chapter 4
IN RHYTHM WITH NATURE

Life—vitality—is a value.
—Dick Price

One autumn morning, I sat on my porch, watching golden leaves drift to the ground. The trees pulsed gently in the wind, their rhythm strangely familiar, like breathing. The air was crisp, the sky wide and blue, and the hush of the season seemed to reach into my chest, soothing the thrum of urgency I hadn't realized I was carrying. All around me, the natural world moved to a rhythm more ancient than thought. Slowly, my own heart began to meet it. In that spacious stillness, I could finally hear what I so often miss: "You belong here, not for what you do, but for who you are—aware, alive, becoming."

In that quiet pause, I touched on a deeper truth that modern life urges us to forget. Nature doesn't rush. It doesn't fear pauses. It doesn't resist endings. It moves in a rhythm of growth and rest, expansion and release, death and renewal. And so do we, if we let ourselves remember.

So much of our modern culture trains us to override these natural cycles. We're encouraged to power through exhaustion, to measure our worth by constant output, and to treat rest as a reward for productivity rather than a rhythm essential to life. We push through what needs time to ripen. We fear the stillness that follows the end. Instead of moving with change, we try to manage or master it.

When we slow down, we reorient. We attune to life's rhythms in our bodies, our relationships, and the world around us, remembering that change has its own pace and its own intelligence. We begin to see that wisdom rarely speaks in commands or strategies but in timing, in sensation, in the subtle invitations life offers to align rather than control.

It is in these moments, in the breath between and in the silence beneath, that we remember we are part of something larger than ourselves. We are not machines built for endless output but living beings meant to move in rhythm with a natural world.

Nowhere is this rhythm more evident than in the seasons themselves.

THE WISDOM OF SEASONS

Nature honors every phase. Spring initiates by awakening possibilities. Summer expands through the fullness of expression. Autumn releases by letting go with grace. And winter rests, withdrawing into stillness to gather resources for what is to come.

This cycle is not only biological and ecological; it is also psychological, emotional, and deeply experiential. It reflects how life moves, not only around us, but through us as well. When we attune to these natural rhythms, both external and internal, we become more resilient, more creative, and more fully alive. We learn to trust the ebb and flow of life: to release what has run its course, to wait when patience is called for, and to act when the moment is ripe. But when we lose touch with these rhythms, we grow brittle. Disconnection takes hold. And soon, we begin to feel depleted, physically, mentally, emotionally, and spiritually.

Fortunately, life continually offers reminders of the cyclical intelligence we've forgotten. Female bodies with functioning ovaries, for example, hold this rhythm in their very biology. Menstrual cycles mirror the moon, the tides, and the natural rise and fall of energy. Across cultures and throughout time, the female body, as typically depicted, has been honored as a living compass, revealing that life moves not in straight lines but in spirals.

Yet modern culture, dominated by a linear, production-driven mindset, tends to pathologize this relational intelligence, often relegating it to the background or medicating it altogether. As a society, we've been taught to suppress what we should revere and to override what we ought to honor. The body's signals are dismissed as inconvenient. Emotional sensitivity is labeled irrational. Stillness is mistaken for laziness. In turning away from these natural rhythms, we sever ourselves from the very source of wisdom that could guide and restore us.

Restoration becomes possible when what has long been held apart is brought back into relationship. When contextual awareness rooted in rhythm, presence, and attunement is met by discernment driven by focus, direction, and purposeful action, a new possibility emerges. Action no longer arises from pressure or fear, but from coherence with life's natural flow.

Presence cultivated at this intersection gives rise to an inner movement aligned with participation in a living system. When our inner experience comes into coherence with the outer world, integration becomes possible. This marks an evolutionary shift from fragmentation toward wholeness, from domination to the embodied rhythm of relational flow.

This is the natural rhythm that lives at the heart of relational intelligence. It is the pulse of the Communal Heart, the dynamic field that invites us to move in sync with one another and with the wider world to which we belong. In this space, rest and renewal are not obstacles to progress. They are essential to it. They remind us that we are not machines but living beings, woven into a web of relationships, shaped by rhythm and sustained by reciprocity. To remember the cycles is to remember ourselves. To remember ourselves is to remember the wisdom of wholeness in our bodies, in our relationships, and in how we meet the world.

THE CYCLE OF COMPLETION

Cyclical intelligence manifests through what is known as the Gestalt Contact Cycle. It describes how experience takes shape in the field of awareness—how sensations, needs, and emotions emerge from the background, seek completion, and then return to rest. We can draw on this framework to help us restore meaning to our actions that have begun to feel automatic or lifeless. This embodied process supports integration and the return to wholeness through eight revolving states of being:[1]

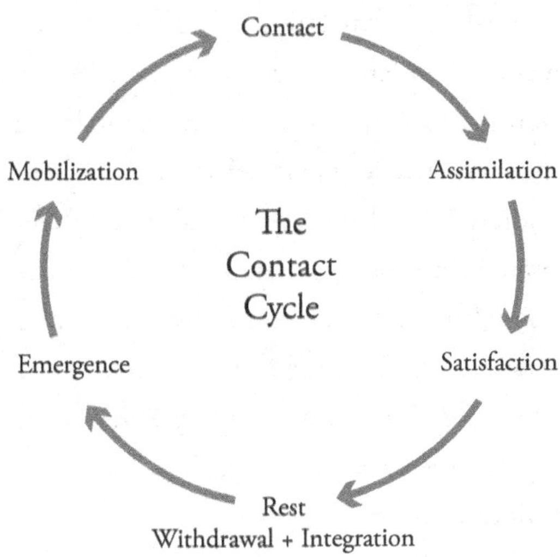

Fig. 4.1. Adapted from Joseph Zinker's Cycle of Experience.[2]

- **Rest:** At the beginning, we are in a quiet state of undifferentiated awareness.
- **Emergence:** A need or impulse begins to surface.
- **Mobilization:** Energy rises, inducing an ability to scan our environment for how to respond.
- **Contact:** Engagement initiates with what we believe will meet the need.
- **Assimilation:** The experience is absorbed or rejected.
- **Satisfaction:** If the need is met, a sense of completion follows.
- **Withdrawal:** The energy softens, and we retreat.
- **Integration:** The experience becomes part of us, and we return to rest.

For example, as I write (rest), I realize my lips are dry, and my mouth is parched (emergence). I get up, pour a glass of water (mobilization), bring it up to my lips, and drink (contact), swallow (assimilation), experience quenched thirst (satisfaction), sit back down (withdrawal), and then return to writing feeling renewed and invigorated (integration), waiting for the next need to arise (rest). Put simply, in response to my feeling of thirst, I shift my frame of awareness from my writing to drinking water and then back to my writing. The act of drinking water satisfies my thirst, which completes the cycle of change, and I am free to return to work without distraction.

Whether in small acts, such as taking a sip of water, or in major life transitions, like ending a relationship or changing careers, this cycle plays out continuously. The more fluidly we move through its phases, the more comfortable we feel and the more whole we become.

HOW WE INTERRUPT OURSELVES

That said, we rarely complete these cycles. More often than not, we interrupt ourselves. We override the need for rest. We rush through emergence. We avoid meaningful contact. We stay busy to escape the discomfort of withdrawal. We may even bypass integration entirely. Instead of completing the cycle, we accumulate what is known as unfinished business, which typically consists of unfelt feelings, unmet needs, unspoken truths, and unlived dreams. This buildup doesn't disappear. It settles into the body, seeps into our relationships, and eventually colors how we experience life itself.

Take Marvin, for instance. He had spent decades in a reliable but uninspiring career in accounting. What truly lit him up was baking. He dreamed of opening a small pastry café, even taking night classes in culinary arts. His eyes would sparkle when he described the perfect croissant or the meditative calm of kneading dough. For years, he researched, planned, and imagined the transition, but he never took the leap. Each time a season of change began to stir within him—each time spring's call to new life emerged, or fall's beaconing to release—fear and self-doubt would interrupt it. He told himself it was too risky, too late, and definitely too indulgent.

So, he stayed in his uninspiring job. He remained dutiful and practical, even as a part of him withered. Time passed, and he eventually retired, wealthy but having never followed his calling. Not long after, Marvin was diagnosed with a terminal illness. During our final sessions, he frequently spoke of that unlived dream, not with bitterness, but with sorrow for the life that might have been. His dream, like those of so many others, remained unfinished, not because it was unworthy, but because it was unmet.

These interruptions don't just break our hearts. They also shape our lives.

Unfinished business lingers in us like static, making it harder to hear our inner knowing and trust our own timing. We begin to feel incomplete, out of rhythm with ourselves, and misaligned with the world around us. We may become haunted by the feeling that something significant was left behind, even if we can't name it exactly.

Unfortunately, this internal fragmentation doesn't stay contained. Fragmented lives give rise to fragmented families, communities, and, ultimately, the systems we create and must live within.

When we cannot complete our own inner cycles of fulfillment, we struggle to participate in the larger cycles of life, including rest, grief, repair, and renewal. As a society, we attempt to build structures for others while remaining out of alignment with ourselves.

If Marvin's story teaches us anything, it is that our longing is not the problem. Our longing is the intelligence of life itself, nudging us toward wholeness.

THE POWER OF AWARENESS

So let us rest here in awareness. Follow along with this simple, embodied practice to expand your capacity for engaging with the senses through awareness.

Take a moment to settle in place, right where you are. When you feel ready, turn your attention toward your breath. Feel it move in, pause, and move out. There's nothing to do. Nowhere to go. Just be here now.

See if you can sense the place where breath and awareness meet, where your awareness meets the breath, and your breath meets awareness. Notice if anything shifts when you do.

Gently bring your awareness to sensation. Feel your body resting in the chair or on the ground. Notice the support beneath you. Sense the temperature of the air, the sounds and smells in the room—perhaps a tingling, an ache, or a pressure inside your body. There's no need to urge anything to change. Just allow sensations to arise within the field of awareness and then return.

Softly ask yourself, "What am I aware of right now?" Try to name the essence of it out loud, if you can, and then let it go.

I invite you to continue: "What about now?"

"And now?"

This simple act of bringing attention to the unfolding of our lived experience begins to mend the gap between our thinking about life and actually living it from the inside out. It reminds us that life is not meant to be mastered but met, moment by moment, again and again.[3]

PRESENCE AS A GATEWAY HOME

This practice of presence—of being here with whatever is present and immediate—is a gateway to the Communal Heart. When we stop striving to manage or improve ourselves and instead turn toward the raw actuality of our lives, a deeper intelligence begins to emerge, expressed as fierce tenderness and a steady willingness to meet our pain, our longings, and our truth with nonjudgmental awareness.

This kind of embodied awareness is not passive; it is participatory. It allows us to stay with what is alive and real without turning away, numbing out, or rushing to fix. When we stop bracing against life, we discover the freedom to choose, and in that freedom, we create the conditions to respond.

Learning to respond is a profound act of courage. As we loosen our grip on how things should be, we become more able to accept what actually is. From this openness, trust begins to grow, not through force, management, or control, but through the practice of attuning first to ourselves and then to our surroundings, including one another. From such attunement, coherence emerges. In other words, to be present and responsive is to be alive within the relational field. It is an invitation to move as a part of a whole, not above or outside it, and to remember that we are not isolated selves but participants in a living web of relationships.

When we honor life's seasons in this way, we begin moving with change rather than against it. In the winter of a situation, we allow ourselves to grieve what is ending without rushing the process. In the spring of an experience, we welcome what is beginning, even when it arrives early or unexpectedly. The unknown is no longer to be feared but embraced as a necessary part of becoming whole.

Over time, this rhythm of attunement becomes a practice, a way of listening that is both embodied and relational. We learn to listen not only to our bodies and inner longings but also to the felt movements of others, such as the emotional tone of a room, the energy between people, and the unspoken language of timing and transition. Attunement reminds us that we are not separate from life but moving with its unfolding. When we tune into the natural cycles within and around us, we are better able to meet life as it is and respond with discernment and care, allowing coherence to emerge in its own time.

In Chapter 5, we'll explore how this deep listening becomes the foundation for presence as a grounded way of being that brings us home to the moment, to each other, and to what gives life its meaning. Here, presence becomes both an anchor and a bridge, anchoring us in the now and bridging us backward and forward in time across the living field of connection that unites us all and everything we touch.

Chapter 5
THE PRACTICE OF BEING HERE

Awareness is the greatest agent for change.
—Eckhart Tolle

In a modern world that moves at the rapid pace of distraction, cultivating the slow, steady quality of presence can feel like a revolutionary act. The modern condition has trained us to live from the neck up, navigating life through thoughts, plans, and problem-solving. This habitual overreliance on the mind alone pulls us out of contact with the richness and immediacy of our lived experience.

Presence asks us to meet life differently.

It invites us into the body, into the breath, and into the felt experience of now. Presence does not demand perfection or performance. Instead, it calls for slowing down, turning inward, and staying with what arises, even when it's uncomfortable or unfamiliar.

Sometimes, engaging with the present is as simple as placing a hand on our chest and feeling the steady rhythm of our heartbeat. Other times, presence shows up when we notice how sunlight warms our skin through a window on an otherwise ordinary afternoon. In such moments, the noise recedes. We exhale, allowing our attention to settle on what is truly needed.

Here, presence is not a technique for paying attention. It is a courageous way of being that loosens the illusion of control we so often hold over our circumstances. It allows us to meet life as it unfolds without grasping, without flinching, and without turning away. In doing so, we create space for what is real and alive, for what is asking to be known around us, and, most importantly, within us. Presence is how we come home to ourselves and to the world we belong to by opening our capacity to sense into the web of relationships that holds us.

TURNING TOWARD WHAT'S REAL

Cultivating presence begins with awareness as a spacious, receptive field that holds us and everything we are a part of. Broadening our attention to rest in this field of awareness enables us to witness without rushing to interpret; to notice without judgment; and to remain attuned to the fullness of experience within us, around us, and in the in-between spaces where meaning arises. Within this spacious field, attention can hold our inner sensations and emotions, our external surroundings, and the realm of thoughts and interpretations, all with curiosity and compassion.

Imagine awareness as light. At times, when the aperture

setting is wide, the light spreads like moonlight—soft, diffuse, and capable of illuminating the entire landscape. In this glow, we sense the mood of a room before a word is spoken, feel the tension behind a loved one's silence, or recognize the faint stirrings of our own intuition. This moonlight, or open awareness, is receptive, relational, and full of texture, allowing us to perceive the emotional contours of a situation, even when they are barely visible.

At other times, attention shapes that light, functioning like a flashlight—sharp, focused, and trained on a single point. This mode of attention helps us solve problems, make decisions, and take action. It is precise, deliberate, and incredibly useful.

Both modes of attention, broad and narrow, are essential. But modern life has taught us to rely almost exclusively on the flashlight beam at the expense of the guidance of the moonlight. In our attempts to analyze, categorize, and problem-solve, we may neglect perceiving the wider field of meaning. We learn to fix but not to feel. To manage, but not to relate. As our focus narrows, the world grows smaller and so do we. We begin to confuse the flashlight for the moonlight, and our inner worlds start to reflect this constriction—what should be a rich and dynamic internal landscape becomes constrained by whatever we concentrate on. We become efficient but unmoored and productive but lonely.

Presence is a way of being that helps restore what has been lost. It invites us to loosen our grip on control and widen the aperture of attention. When we do, it opens the lens to the relational field, the living intelligence that arises through contact and attunement. It is the difference between thinking about life and actually touching and being touched by it. In this space, meaning is not constructed but revealed, gently and often quietly, through our willingness to simply be with what is.

ATTENTION IS NOT NEUTRAL

Think of a time when someone truly listened to you, not just nodded politely or waited for their turn to speak, but listened with their full, undivided attention. Their presence was steady, open, and attuned. You likely softened. You felt seen, heard, and even met. You may have noticed your breath deepening, an inner letting go, your shoulders dropping as tension released. In that moment, you were no longer carrying the weight of your burdens all alone. You felt safer, more real, and more connected.

Now think of a time when someone was physically there but mentally elsewhere. They were distracted, perhaps checking their phone or preoccupied with their own internal monologue. The quality of the connection probably lessened. The conversation may have continued, but the felt sense of being together faded. A vital thread in the relational field between you two began to fray.

Attention is not neutral. Depending on how it is offered, it can nourish or deplete, attune or alienate. When attention rests within a wide field of awareness—when broad, contextual awareness remains open while focused attention engages—we create a space where stillness can give rise to truth and where something beyond words can be felt, held, and integrated.

In essence, presence invites aliveness. It welcomes what has been silenced to speak aloud, what has been hidden to emerge, and what has been bracing to finally exhale. In a world saturated with distraction, absorbed by the fallout of the metacrisis, offering our undivided attention is more than a courtesy. It is an act of love.

THE DANCE OF ATTENTION

As we have already begun to explore, how we attend to life—how we perceive, engage, and respond—is shaped by widely shared archetypal patterns, often described as feminine and masculine. These energies are expressions of psychic and embodied tendencies that influence how we inhabit our bodies, relate to others, and make meaning. They are not rigid roles or gendered prescriptions, but living relational orientations, and therefore ways of participating in life, that exist within each of us. The feminine mode of attending inclines toward receptivity. It listens, holds, nurtures, and attunes to context, relationship, and nuance. The masculine mode of attending inclines toward agency. It differentiates, directs, structures, and aims toward purposeful action.

In other words, the feminine gravitates toward wholeness and relational coherence, while the masculine gravitates toward differentiation, direction, and form. Both modes find embodiment through attention—broad awareness and focused attention—and both are necessary. When integrated, they support our full humanity.

However, in lived experience, these archetypal tendencies—toward receptive presence on the one hand and problem-solving action on the other—often appear with different emphasis in females and males, even as both capacities are present, to varying degrees, in every human being.[1] This difference becomes especially visible in cisgender, heterosexual couples and never more so than in moments of distress.

In my therapy practice, during times of difficulty, many women voice a longing to be listened to without interruption, to be received rather than treated as problems to be solved. What frequently unfolds is not a lack of care, but a mismatch in how care is expressed and received. Many men, who have been developmentally and culturally shaped to equate care with fixing, often struggle to respond in this way, unsure whether stillness and presence can truly be enough. Yet when these men begin to weave presence into their sense of doing, blending broad, contextual awareness with focused, purposeful engagement, they usually discover a fuller capacity for connection. What once felt like inaction becomes a powerful form of support. In learning to stay present without immediately acting, they discover that presence itself is a form of participation, not withdrawal. In that shift, new awareness opens, both within themselves and in the relational space between them and their partners.

At other times, I have observed a complementary pattern emerge. Many women are deeply attuned to relational undercurrents and emotional nuance, sensing what is unfolding beneath the surface. However, this sensitivity can sometimes come at the cost of fully inhabiting their own agency. In an effort to preserve harmony or remain responsive to others, women may hesitate to name their needs directly, set clear boundaries, or take decisive steps on their own behalf. When these women begin to integrate more focused attention and assertiveness into their relational awareness—learning to speak clearly, act decisively, and tolerate the discomfort that can accompany self-advocacy—they often discover a new kind of strength. Presence no longer requires self-erasure, and care no longer depends solely on accommodation. In this shift, purposeful action becomes an expression of self-respect, and relationships gain clarity, vitality, and resilience. What once felt like disruption becomes a pathway to trust, forming within both themselves and the relational space they share with others.

Because these differences are often felt somatically as shifts in energy, pace, or tone, they can generate tension, particularly in intimate relationships, where either partner may unconsciously assume the other person shares their preferred way of attending to and participating in the world. Yet this friction reveals a profound opportunity for integration. When we begin to honor the other's way of orienting and engaging, while cultivating a more nuanced awareness of our own habitual patterns of attention and participation—balancing both the receptive capacity of the feminine and the agentic direction of the masculine—we stop outsourcing wholeness to another. We grow more balanced and mature. Attention becomes less of a task to perform and more a presence to embody. It becomes a dynamic dance of listening and responding, yielding and acting, receiving and offering.

In this integration lies the beginning of a new way of relating, one centered less on roles or reflexes and more on embodied awareness. When we learn to meet life with both tenderness and discernment, and depth and direction, we begin to inhabit the full spectrum of our humanity and, with it, a deeper intimacy with the world around us.

OUR ABILITY TO RESPOND

When our attention is balanced, we can meet life as it is. From here, awareness becomes more available, choice returns, trust grows, and responsiveness becomes attuned rather than reactive. This is the shift that turns the dance of attention into a relational dance with reality itself. Let's explore each of these phenomena more closely.[2]

Awareness: As we've explored earlier in this chapter, awareness comes first as the spacious, receptive field that, when embodied, becomes presence. It is the receptive holding capacity often associated with the feminine.

Choice: Within embodied awareness comes the conscious pivot that allows for aligned action. It is the capacity to pause, discern, and respond in ways that honor what matters most in each moment. Rather than reacting from habit or fear, choice invites intentionality. This is the agentic function often associated with the masculine, one that is focused, directed, and deliberate.

Trust: Trust is the felt confidence in the body's natural intelligence. It is the ability to regulate and orient in relationship to life, arising when awareness and choice move together in harmony. In practice, it shows up as the instinct to step forward when the moment calls and to settle in place when stillness is needed. Trust reflects our willingness to be changed by what we encounter. It lives in the rhythm between knowing and not knowing, between surrender and devotion.

Responsiveness: When awareness, choice, and trust converge, an embodied expression arises. Responsiveness is how we meet the moment with integrity—self-regulating, co-regulating with others, and attuning to the greater field of which we are part. This is what restores our sense of relational wholeness. Wholeness cannot be forced. It can only be remembered by returning to the rhythm that lives within, between, and among us.

You can feel the embodied difference in these different ways of being if you have ever watched a child learning to ride a bike. At first, you hang back, watchful, so that they can find their own balance. That is awareness. But when the handlebars begin to wobble and they lean too far, you recognize that you have a choice: step in with support or hold back and let them develop their own. Then, at a certain point, you see they've reached their edge. You extend a steadying hand. That is responsiveness, born from trust in your ability to meet the moment, to sense what the situation requires, and to respond accordingly.

Awareness, choice, and trust, culminating in responsiveness, are necessary for relating well. Without awareness, we fall into habit or reactivity. Without choice, our responses aren't truly ours; they are reflexes shaped by the past. Without trust, we lose our sense of belonging to ourselves, to others, and to the unfolding of life. Without responsiveness, we cling to the illusion of control and struggle to believe that our actions have any real impact.

This relational dance is what makes cultivating presence trustworthy. It allows us to meet others and ourselves, not with a script, but with sincerity. It is how we offer steadiness without intrusion and care without control. Presence is the ground from which healing becomes possible, not because we've fixed or solved, but because we've shown up fully, openly, and without pretense.

SLOWING DOWN TO NOTICE

I remember once walking through my neighborhood, caught in a swirl of thoughts. A stressful conversation replayed in my mind, looping on repeat. My attention was fragmented, split between past regrets and future worries, barely anchored in the present.

Then I shifted. I paused. Took a slow breath and let my awareness settle downward, from my head and through my body. I experienced my breathing begin to steady. Then I began to notice what was around me: the amber light of the setting sun filtering through the clouds, the distant laughter of children playing in a backyard, and the firmness of the sidewalk underneath my feet. Just ahead, a neighbor struggled to carry his grocery bags. Had I stayed distracted in my thoughts, I might have passed him by without even noticing. But presence revealed the opportunity. I walked over and offered to help. He looked up, surprised, and then broke into a smile. We shared a brief interaction, nothing dramatic, only a simple exchange. And yet something meaningful happened. A small thread of connection wove itself between us.

This is how presence reshapes the world, through everyday moments of attunement. When we slow down enough to notice, feel, and respond, life opens. In that opening, something sacred can emerge.

However, what shapes our experience is not only where our

attention rests, but also the *quality* of our attending—the subtle texture through which reality comes into view. To fully grasp the power of presence, we must turn toward perception itself: the invisible lens through which we filter experience, make meaning, and determine what we allow in and what we leave out.

HOW PERCEPTION SHAPES THE WORLD

Presence and perception are intimately connected. Gestalt psychology helps us understand this through the dynamic relationship between figure and background. The figure is what stands out. It is what catches our focus in any given moment. The ground is the broader context, or the relational field from which that figure emerges. Both modes of attention are necessary for us to perceive the world coherently. Yet most of the time in modern society we focus on the figure, forgetting that the ground gives it meaning.

According to Iain McGilchrist, the left hemisphere of the brain tends to privilege figure: It parses, analyzes, and isolates parts. The right hemisphere, in contrast, is more attuned to ground: It senses context, relationship, and the integrated whole. To truly understand something, we first need to sense it through the right hemisphere, where direct, lived knowing begins. That knowing is then passed to the left hemisphere, where it is given form through words, ideas, or categories. Finally, this explanation is brought back to the right hemisphere to determine whether it remains faithful to what was first known. If it does, it settles into a deeper understanding. If it does not, we let it go and remain open to a truer picture.[3]

However, when we privilege the figure alone, fixating on isolated details while losing sight of the larger field, we disconnect from a fuller, more nuanced sense of meaning. Meaning does not live in the figure or the ground; it arises in the *relationship* between them. It emerges in the dance between part and whole, between narrow, focused attention, often associated with the left hemisphere, and broad, contextual awareness, more strongly emphasized by the right hemisphere.

A helpful example is the well-known rabbit-duck illusion.[4] This single image can be seen as either a rabbit or a duck, but not both at once. Try it yourself.

Fig. 5.1. Rabbit-duck illusion.

The shift from one to the other does not happen because the image changes, but because our perception shifts. The ground we unconsciously reference changes, and suddenly we see differently.

This capacity to shift our attention is a profound aspect of presence. It allows us to move fluidly between perspectives, relaxing our grip on fixed interpretations and opening us to the interplay between distinction and context, self and other, and figure and field. To live this way deepens meaning. It is to see not only with the eyes but with the whole of our aware attention, so that we begin to perceive not just what stands before us but also what holds and shapes it.

Let's consider another example of a toddler standing alone on a sidewalk. At first glance, you might feel a surge of alarm—your attention narrows, interpreting the scene as one of potential danger or abandonment. Moments later, you see a parent rushing out from a nearby house to embrace the toddler. The situation has not changed, but your perception has. The meaning of the moment—the Gestalt—shifts, not because the figure (the toddler) changed but because the ground (the context) came into view. This is the relational nature of perception. It is never fixed or isolated. It is always shaped by what surrounds it, what precedes it, and what lies just beyond the edges of what we think we see.

Presence makes perceptual shifts possible. It moves us from fragmented looking to contextual seeing, from isolation to relationship, and from knee-jerk reactivity to a grounded coherence. As we do, presence widens our perceptual lens, allowing us to perceive not only the individual parts but also the larger whole to which we belong. From this widened perception, choice becomes possible.

MIDWIFING RELATIONAL WISDOM

Because our modern culture trains us to narrow and sharpen our focus in order to fix, it frequently rewards efficiency at the expense of depth. A popular, contemporary business phrase, "move fast and break things," comes to mind. Yet wisdom rarely arises from the same narrow attention that drives our grasping for control. More often, it comes through restraint, not as passivity but as presence, which involves witnessing, allowing, honoring, and accepting the slow unfolding of what is alive and real in that given moment. In this way, cultivating wisdom is akin to midwifing. Just as a midwife accompanies a laboring mother and child through the uncertainty of birth, so too does a broad, contextual attention accompany the emergence of insight. Wisdom is less a product of force and more a fruit of listening. It arises when we relax our grip and widen our attention to include the whole of what is present.

This spacious stance, frequently associated with the feminine, is one that many in our world, whether they realize it or not, are aching to reclaim. It arises when we sense nuance, attend to context, and allow meaning to surface organically from the conditions we inhabit. When this receptive orientation is integrated with the masculine capacity for focus, direction, and purposeful action, something transformative begins to take shape. We shift from reaction to response, from dominance to coherence, and, perhaps most importantly, from performance to participation, as we tune into a natural rhythm already pulsing within us, waiting to be sensed, trusted, and lived rather than imposed.

This is the relational movement, it seems to me, that we are being called into. The call is urgent. We don't just need clever strategies or reactive solutions to manage the interwoven challenges of our times. We need relational wisdom—the deep, grounded responsiveness that emerges most reliably from balanced attention and integrated modes of attending. Our full attention draws not only on the focused precision of doing but also on the spacious receptivity of being. Together, these complementary ways of knowing open a way of meeting life that doesn't distort life through the lens of dominance or the illusion of control but widens our capacity to see more fully and respond wisely to life as it is.

When we begin to live this way, an internal transformation occurs. The more we cultivate presence, the more attuned we become to what lies beneath our habitual defenses. We notice the ways we brace against life, rush past ourselves, or numb what feels too tender to face. Gradually, we learn to yield instead—to stay, breathe, and remain aware. From this embodied awareness, a more relational intelligence begins to emerge, one that knows how to respond to what the situation requires with both discernment and care.

While presence opens the door, it is our inner work that steadies our path toward wholeness. We must turn inward, tend to the wounds and stories we carry, and begin the healing that allows us to stay connected, not just in fleeting moments but over time and even under pressure. In Chapter 6, we'll explore how this inner work becomes the fertile ground in which relational wisdom takes root within us, between us, and as part of the wider relational field we share.

Chapter 6

REWRITING THE STORIES WE INHERIT

True transformation is not about becoming something else; it is about becoming more fully ourselves. It is about peeling away the layers of fear and conditioning that obscure the truth of who we are.
—Russ Hudson

Beneath the surface of every human relationship lies an unspoken story. These stories are shaped by our early experiences, by needs that went unmet, and by the ways we learned to stay safe in a world that could not consistently receive us. They are the internalized agreements we made with ourselves about what could be felt, what had to be ignored, and what it would take to be loved and belong.

Inner work is the practice of turning toward these stories with compassion, not to judge or fix them, but to witness, to understand, and, perhaps, to rewrite them. To sincerely connect with others, we must first come home to ourselves, which means nurturing a tenderness toward our earliest wounds and deep-seated narratives. We must remember that this is not a solo quest for self-improvement, but a journey of befriending all of who we are as an intimate and courageous act of self-acceptance. When we begin to see our inner landscapes more clearly, we loosen the grip of old patterns and open space for new ways of relating to ourselves and one another.

Consider Irene, a client in her forties. On the surface, she was thriving; she had a successful career and a steady relationship. But inwardly, she carried a persistent anxiety and a body perpetually braced for impact. "I feel like I'm always waiting for the other shoe to drop," she confided one day.

Over time, we uncovered a childhood marked by criticism and emotional volatility. In her early parental environment, vulnerability was dangerous. Expressing needs consistently led to shame. As a result, Irene's nervous system had adapted, remaining in a state of high alert. Even decades later, her vigilance lingered, embedded in her posture, her breathing, and her underlying diminished sense of self.

Even so, cultivating presence began to change her inner terrain. Slowly, she learned to stay with her internal discomfort rather than distract herself from it. She practiced breathing into the tightness, noticing the flutter of fear, and grounding herself in the present moment. Gradually, she came to trust that her inner experience could be welcomed and held. In that welcoming, she began to relax and move from reactivity toward responsiveness.

This is a way toward integration and into the field of belonging.

Irene's story reveals how developing embodied awareness can help us witness old patterns with compassion. With time, this compassionate witnessing becomes the fertile ground from which new stories—and ultimately, new ways of being—can emerge, rooted in attunement, coherence, and the dynamic, relational intelligence of the Communal Heart.

CONFRONTING OUR INNER LANDSCAPE

Unresolved childhood experiences commonly leave behind unacknowledged beliefs about our worth, our place in the world, and whether it is safe to be fully ourselves.[1] These beliefs become internal narratives, shaping how we interpret events and how we show up in our relationships. Without conscious awareness of them, we may find ourselves reacting not to what is happening now but to the echo of unfinishedness that still lives in the body and colors our current experience with the past.

In my own life, the early message I received was unmistakable: "Be strong, be capable, and, above all, handle everything by yourself!" I was consistently praised for my independence and tenacity. As a result, I learned to hold my life together on my own, even under the toughest circumstances. So I continued in this way until the day I couldn't any longer.

Motherhood cracked me open, followed by years of single parenting, both of which laid my early survival strategies bare. The relentlessness of tending to others, in my private practice and at home, while carrying everything without much support, revealed how much I had internalized the belief that love meant self-sacrifice and that worth depended on accomplishing everything and doing it well.

One evening, I sat in silence with my phone in my hand. I felt the weight of shame as a lump rising in my throat, the ache of admitting that I was struggling and could not take another step. Then I remembered a piece of advice a mentor once gave me: "Your strength is not measured by how much you can endure alone, but by how fully you allow yourself to be seen and supported."

This insight changed everything.

Little by little, I began to let people in. I learned to say, "I'm overwhelmed," and to ask, "Can you help?" What surprised me was that sharing my vulnerability didn't diminish me; it expanded me. I came to realize that connection had always been available. I had simply been standing outside it, convinced that I needed to prove myself through self-sufficiency.

Whether our inner work calls us to lean into support or to stand more firmly in our own strength, the process is the same: reclaiming the parts of ourselves we exiled early on to meet the expectations of those we depended on.[2] However, true integration doesn't mean becoming perfect. It means becoming whole. It means restoring our capacity to relate to the present moment rather than react to the wounds of the past.

MEETING FEAR WITH CURIOSITY

Even with the best of intentions, we can get stuck, and more often than not, it is fear that keeps us from moving forward—fear of rejection, of failure, of being too much or not enough. Fear has a way of reinforcing the very patterns we most long to outgrow. It keeps us tethered to familiar survival strategies, even when they no longer serve us. Real change, therefore, calls us to meet fear with curiosity, to listen for what it is trying to protect, and then, with gentleness and compassion, to choose to move forward anyway.

Many of our most entrenched patterns can be traced back to internalized messages we absorbed in childhood, messages that form the basis for how we protect what was once most vulnerable within us.[3] These messages may include beliefs such as the following:

- Mistakes are unacceptable. You must always get it right.
- Your needs are a burden. Focus on others first.
- Something fundamental is missing. Continue searching for what will make life special.
- Emotions are dangerous. Stay agreeable.
- Struggle means you're doing something worthwhile. Ease is suspect.
- Needing help is a weakness. Handle it yourself.
- Your value depends on your success. Keep producing to stand out.
- The world is uncertain. Stay alert and find support.
- Pain will trap you. Stay positive and don't look back.

These beliefs don't always stem from overt trauma. More often, they set in gradually through repeated misattunements, social conditioning, or the ways we learned who we needed to be and how we needed to behave in order to belong to our original families. Over the course of our lives, these unconscious relational contracts mold who we think we are, influence how we relate to others, and define the edges of what we believe is possible.

But these beliefs are not the whole truth of who we are. They are adaptations—intelligent, protective, and necessary at the time they formed. And because they were learned, they can also be unlearned, and with awareness, they can be transformed.

We can shift the unconscious patterns we carry by tracing the origins of the stories that underlie our behaviors. As we examined in the previous section, each of us internalized messages early in life, long before we had words for them. These messages shape the strategies we use to remain safe and belong, forming the lens through which we perceive the present. By noticing how these strategies influence our attention, we also become aware of what escapes our notice now. From here, we can reflect on what is true for us in this moment and consider what new message might more accurately reflect who we are and what we need today. Embracing such a new message can shift our perspective and reshape how we respond.[4]

Try it and take your time. These shifts rarely happen overnight. Each time we bring a hidden pattern into awareness, we create just enough space to choose our responses differently. We begin to loosen our grip on old scripts and, in their place, discover a new way of relating from presence rather than fear-fueled protection. This is how inner work becomes liberation, moving us from who we are into who we are becoming.

HEALING THROUGH ANOTHER

The path of inner work is neither linear nor final. There is no fixed endpoint, only a continual unfolding. Each time we turn toward what is difficult to face, we become less guarded and more available, less entangled in the past and more attuned to the present moment. Through this ongoing process, we begin to reclaim the parts of ourselves we once rejected or disowned. In that reclamation, we become more trustworthy, not only to ourselves but also to others. What once seemed unlovable—our fears, our wounds, and even our longings—no longer stands as a barrier to connection. Instead, the inner core of who we are becomes a bridge, forging a way to greater understanding and mutual compassion.

This is the paradox of healing. The very places that once held shame and separation become precious, fertile ground for intimacy. In its own way, inner work is both a private endeavor and an act of service. It is a personal movement toward coherence that extends outward, shaping the quality of our relationships, strengthening the resiliency of our communities, and supporting the healing of our broader culture.

In essence, though inner work may feel very personal, it is never truly solitary. Like all of life, healing happens in relationship, especially through another. We need others who don't rush to fix or offer solutions but instead know how to hold space for our becoming, those who can stay present in the face of discomfort and remind us, again and again, that we don't have to carry it all alone. Whether it is a therapist, a soul friend, or a trusted group of people, these companions become living mirrors. They help us see what we cannot yet see in ourselves. They steady us through the turbulence of transformation. And perhaps most profoundly, they show us that vulnerability is not a weakness but a path into fuller connection and shared humanity.

This is how we find our way into the Communal Heart: through presence, attunement, and the sacred space that exists between ourselves and others. When we learn to meet ourselves with tenderness, we are able to expand our capacity to meet others with that same compassion. Integration, then, is not merely an internal unfolding. It is a communal response, one that invites a return to trust and, ultimately, a return to love.

In Part III, we'll explore how the inner work of integration lays the foundation for a life grounded in connection because healing breathes through the space between us. It lives in the relational field where *Me* widens to include *We*.

An Invitation to Practice the Communal Heart in Daily Life

The Communal Heart emerges as a way of responding to life when we balance broad, contextual awareness with narrow, focused attention—being with doing, connection with separation, and togetherness with autonomy. Every moment offers a chance to practice this integration.

Check-In: Are You Aligning?

Take a moment to ask yourself the following:

- Where is my attention right now?
- What happens when I soften my attention and simply notice what is here? In sensation? In feeling? In thought? And through my senses as I experience my surroundings?
- Can I stay with my experience long enough to begin to recognize what this moment asks of me?

Bringing our awareness to these questions invites us into presence. From presence, we realign within ourselves, with each other, and with the natural rhythm of the Communal Heart.

Part III

RETURNING TO ONE ANOTHER

Chapter 7

THOSE WHO HELP US BECOME

A friend is a loved one who awakens your life in order to free the wild possibilities within you.
—John O'Donohue

Avery and Leo had been together for over fifteen years. They loved each other, but their love was sustained by habit rather than by the generative process of relational intimacy that develops from knowing and being known. By the time they came to therapy, their relationship had grown stale. "It's like we're roommates," Avery said. They were polite and functional, but beneath the surface lived a persistent ache, a longing for connection, for aliveness, but most of all, to be truly seen.

I suggested we begin with presence. I invited them to find their breath and to notice the space where their awareness meets their breath and their breath meets awareness. From there, I asked them to speak just one sentence at a time, followed by a conscious pause to make room for their inner and outer experiences. I recommended they look into each other's eyes while doing this, without rushing, and listen without preparing a response.

They said they felt awkward at first. However, slowly, the tension between them began to release. Tears welled up as their shoulders relaxed. Then, a tender realization emerged: "We've been missing each other while living side by side."

This is what can happen in the relational space between us when we choose to enter it with intention and vulnerability. Nourishment can begin to flow, uniquely human and profoundly healing. Although healing begins within, it is tested and refined in relationship to others. Inner work prepares us to show up differently with greater presence, better attunement, and an expanded capacity for connection, but it is within the space between us that these inner shifts fully take hold. In the mirror of the other, we begin to see ourselves more clearly. In the ebb and flow of authentic contact, our growth becomes embodied, not only understood but also lived out.

This is where the transformational power of intimacy reveals itself.

As Avery and Leo's experience shows, we tend to think of intimacy as closeness, as the narrowing of distance between self and other. But the intimacy at the center of the Communal Heart is not defined by physical proximity alone. It is defined by the willingness to bridge psychological space. True intimacy, therefore, does not depend on sameness or constant agreement. It arises from our capacity to honor *both* similarity *and* difference: how our personal traits, interests, and values align and how they diverge in novel and meaningful ways. In essence, intimacy lives in the place where we remain rooted in ourselves while reaching toward another.

To hold the tension between ourselves and others while remaining open to vulnerability, we need clear, compassionate boundaries that keep us from mistaking the act of merging—or the blending of our identity with another's feelings and needs—for relational intimacy. Only then can we begin to inhabit that precious middle ground where autonomy and togetherness coexist, where the healing we cultivate within is no longer confined to our private world but extended outward to the world we all share, received and sustained through the courageous process of knowing and being known. That is love.

As our lives remind us, entering the space between us is not easy, and it is almost always messy, which is why we must proceed carefully. But first, we must locate trust.

WHY TRUST IS ESSENTIAL

The space between us is rarely neutral or clear. It is shaped by our histories and is colored by the early experiences that taught us how safe, or unsafe, closeness could be. For some, these imprints create a tendency to move compulsively toward others, driven by a fear of abandonment. For others, the instinct is to stand back at the first sign of vulnerability, afraid of being engulfed or of losing a sense of self.

As we explored previously, these patterns are not personal flaws but adaptive survival strategies, learned behaviors that once protected us in relationships long before we had the tools to navigate them consciously. At the time, they served us well. Yet, if left unexamined, they continue to operate in the background, pulling us out of the present and constricting our capacity to meet life with openness and creativity, especially amid difficulty.

Embodied awareness is the first step in healing. It illuminates what once felt invisible and gives us language for what has long remained unnamed. To move beyond these old patterns, we must be willing to risk closeness. And for that, we need trust in ourselves, in the moment, and in the possibility of connection, even when it once felt unsafe. Trust is the soil in which intimacy grows, allowing us to open, reveal ourselves, and be changed through relationships beyond the boundaries of our skin. Without trust, the space between us remains guarded, an arena of caution rather than mutual transformation.

I once worked with a client named Terrence, who had been in a long-term committed relationship. For years, he had entrusted his romantic partner with the most vulnerable parts of himself—his hopes, dreams, fears, and doubts. In a devastating turn, it was revealed that his partner had been having an affair with his closest friend. The betrayal obviously cut deep. Terrence divorced and entered therapy, uncertain how to move on from this rupture.

At first, he didn't realize how the experience had shaped him. He thought he was recovering and establishing new connections, but gradually, he began to notice he had walled off his inner life. Outwardly, he told himself he was still open. In truth, he let others come only so close.

One evening, after a particularly difficult day, Terrence found himself at a crossroads. He longed for love and support, but a familiar voice in his head warned not to let himself be hurt again. Still, his need for companionship overrode his fear of getting hurt again. With growing awareness and a tentative sense of renewed trust in himself, he decided to ask a new friend, someone he was beginning to feel close to, out on a date. That evening, before opening up to her about something deeply personal, he paused and asked, "Can I trust you with this?"

That moment marked a turning point for him, not because it erased his fear but because he honored his need for safety while still choosing to risk connection. From then on, he began to understand that trust is not blind faith but a slow, discerning process, a learning of who can hold us with care. Perhaps more importantly, when that care is absent or no longer feels consistent, he learned how to trust himself to move to safer ground.

What Terrence's story reveals is that, regardless of our circumstances or what they have been, trust takes courage, especially in the wake of betrayal. While trust is fragile and can be broken quickly, it can also be rebuilt through small, consistent acts of presence and mutual respect. As Terrence discovered, healing isn't about avoiding the risk of being hurt. It's about stepping into relationships with open eyes, clear boundaries, and the willingness to try again, believing the outcome can be different from what it was before.

WHEN PRESENCE BECOMES MUTUAL

While trust lays the foundation for safety, presence nourishes and sustains the connection. Just as presence is essential to personal transformation, it is also the lifeblood of mutuality. Without it, even the most well-intentioned relationships can feel hollow. However, when presence is offered, it becomes a gift of full attention and genuine availability, a powerful and increasingly rare signal that says, "I see you because you matter to me."

I remember a particularly touching exchange with my husband after a long and difficult day. We sat across from each other at dinner, but I was distracted, weighed down by an unacknowledged tension. He noticed and leaned in, not to offer a solution, but to simply be with me. His presence was steady and unhurried.

As I began to speak, I felt myself relax. The air between us seemed to shift. I was no longer alone in my experience. When I had finished, I turned to him and asked, "How did that land for you?" That small question continued to establish a connection and a sense of mutuality. He began to share his own reflections, not to move the focus away from me but to join me in that space of our shared humanity. Together, we entered a field of communion by staying present to what was vital and real for each of us as well as between us.

This is the power of presence in relationship to others. It has the capacity to transform ordinary exchanges into transformative ones. It allows us to see and be seen while becoming more fully alive together in the process.

What this experience between my husband and me also revealed was that the holding quality associated with the feminine archetype—the ability to create a sense of safety without rushing to fix or solve—is not bound by gender. It lives in all of us. When we intentionally cultivate it, offer it to others, and allow ourselves to receive it in return, our relationships become spaces of healing rather than performance.

In these moments, our interactions begin to reflect the natural rhythm of integration itself, as the ongoing dance between doing and being, between action and receptivity, between the focused discernment of the left hemisphere and the contextual awareness of the right. When presence is both offered and received, growth becomes not only possible but inevitable.

CONNECTIONS THAT GROW US

However, not all relationships are meant to hold the depth we may long for. Some connections are inherently transactional, driven by convenience or necessity. Others are circumstantial, emerging from the context of work, location, or shared interests. And yet, there are the rare, transformative connections we might call soul friendships that shape us at the core of who we are.

In the Celtic tradition, a soul friend is more than a companion.[1] They are someone with whom we share a sacred bond, someone who sees us, not simply the parts we choose to reveal, but the whole of who we are. Soul friends reflect both our light and our shadow. They hold us in love while also challenging us to grow into fuller expressions of ourselves.

Two years ago, I founded an international community called Wisdom Exchange, or WE, for short. What began as an intimate online gathering of a few people from around the world, each drawn by a shared longing for meaningful conversation, has gradually evolved into a living field of relational practice. In this space, we do more than share ideas. We practice presence, cultivate mutuality, and experience coherence. We stay with one another through discomfort. We mirror what is hard to see in ourselves. And we call each other forward from mutual respect and, ultimately, from love.

Soul friends are rare. When we find them, they are like a healing salve for the heart. They are the ones we turn to when the world feels too heavy. The ones who remind us who we are when we forget. They walk with us, not ahead or behind, but faithfully beside us, even when the going gets rough. And we do the same for them. Soul friends offer us a nurturing space in which to learn how to grow whole.

THE POSSIBILITY OF RELATIONAL INTIMACY

Of course, relational intimacy does not mean ease. The closer we become to someone, physically and psychologically, the more likely we will inadvertently "step on their toes" and they on ours, so to speak. However, in a culture that regularly confuses agreement with genuine closeness, we are rarely taught how to remain present when things become uncomfortable. Conflict, misunderstanding, and difference are not signs of failure. On the contrary, they are inevitable features of any real relationship. To navigate this complex interpersonal terrain, we must be willing to slow down and choose curiosity over certainty. We must be able to make space for silence, for strong emotion, and for the beautiful, messy work of being human together.

Imagine communities where people can do just that. Where they aren't posturing to impress but practicing how to relate.

Where disagreement isn't a threat to connection but a doorway to greater understanding. Where conflict is no longer treated as a rupture to avoid but as an opportunity to develop trust, truth, and wholeness.

I'm beginning to sense that this is the shape of a new cultural paradigm emerging beneath the crumbling structures of modern life—a paradigm no longer driven by dominance, performance, or control, but rooted in mutual presence, shared coherence, and a collective commitment to fairness and care. Arising from the relational intelligence of the Communal Heart, this paradigm is meant to guide us through the metacrisis, inviting us to reimagine and reshape our systems together in service of a more life-affirming future.

In Chapter 8, we'll explore how this intelligence comes alive through the practice of dialogue, through listening, reflecting, and co-creating meaning together. In a fragmented world, what we need most is not more argument or persuasion but the courage to meet one another in the space between and be willing to listen and speak from the heart.

Chapter 8

THE ART OF GENERATIVE EXCHANGE

The kind of conversation I'm interested in is one in which you start with a willingness to emerge as a slightly different person.
—Theodore Zeldin

I imagine you can recall a conversation that changed you, an interaction in which your defenses came down and you surrendered the need for certainty, leaning instead toward the unknown. You may not have emerged with definitive answers, but you came away with something more valuable—a sense of having been reshaped by the encounter. These meetings are not ordinary exchanges. They are transformative openings that touch an essential quality in us.

And yet, such moments have become increasingly rare.

In today's fast-paced world, as we are caught in crisis after crisis, conversations are frequently reduced to transactions. We speak to be heard, to persuade, to assert a point, and once satisfied, we move on. Sound bites replace substance. Certainty replaces curiosity. And in the rush to respond, we rely on ways to communicate status rather than integrity.

Beneath the noise of distraction and the rush of productivity, a different possibility remains: a way of speaking and listening that invites connection, creativity, and, above all, emergence. Dialogue begins here.

Dialogue is not merely the exchange of ideas. It is an act of relational presence and reciprocal engagement. While it may be anchored in lived experience or inspired by our highest ideals, dialogue ultimately creates a space where difference is not feared or overcome but welcomed as a source of richness and depth. In this way, dialogue is a creative act that invites us to risk being changed by one another. It calls forth curiosity and humility, allowing us to pause our certainty long enough to wonder what else might be true.

This is the essence of generative dialogue. It is a way of meeting that brings us more fully into contact with one another and with our surroundings.

THE PROMISE OF DIALOGUE

I recently witnessed this generative, interpersonal process unfold in a Wisdom Exchange gathering. Maya and Isaac were discussing the role of institutions in organizing culture. Maya, skeptical of institutional power, spoke from a place of personal pain shaped by her family's history of being harmed by systems meant to offer protection. Isaac, on the other hand, had spent much of his life in public service. He spoke with heartfelt conviction about institutional integrity, recalling experiences when these systems had protected order and the well-being of his community.

At first, the room felt tense. Their perspectives seemed irreconcilable, and for a brief time, it looked as if the conversation might slide into defensiveness or even disengagement entirely. Then someone in the group asked, "Would each of you be willing to share the personal experiences that inform your view?"

That question changed everything.

Held by the community's presence and by the trust we had established among us, each began to speak from a more vulnerable place. From here, their pain and truth could find belonging. Soon, the beginnings of what might have pulled them apart began to connect. Maya's voice trembled as she recounted the memory of watching her mother be denied medical care. The room grew still. Isaac listened, not to refute or debate, but to understand. When it was his turn, he shared how a local fire department once saved his childhood home from burning down. Neither spoke from abstract ideology, but from the well of lived experience. In turn, they shifted from debate into dialogue.

They didn't reach an agreement, nor did they need to. What emerged instead was a richer conclusion—a shared sense of each other's humanity. One participant later described what happened between them as "difference without conflict." In a society that increasingly mistakes heated exchange for credibility, we do not have to collapse into sameness, nor do we need to escalate into opposition. Instead, we can learn to carefully hold tension, creating a space that honors diverse experiences and perspectives, and arrive at a fuller, more integrated understanding.

This is the promise that dialogue offers us.

WHAT MAKES DIALOGUE GENERATIVE

Every dialogue is unique, guided by the people involved, the context they are in, and the circumstances that surround them. Yet certain principles can help create the conditions for greater honesty and new possibilities to emerge.

Presence: When we show up fully, not only with our words, but also with our undivided attention, we communicate,"I'm here with you," even in silence.

Curiosity: When we wonder rather than assume, we invite questions like "What shaped your viewpoint?" And without judgment, ask, "What might I be missing? Help me understand?" Curiosity creates space where defensiveness might otherwise set in.

Suspension of Assumptions: When we practice holding our own perspectives lightly by remaining open to surprise and letting go of the need to be right, we make room for what may be true.

I/Thou Orientation: When we engage others as whole, complex beings, not simply as roles, identities, or representatives of an idea, something new can form between us, something greater than the sum of our individual perspectives combined.[1]

Appreciating Similarity and Difference: When we hold the tension between commonality and novelty, we welcome the places where we align and those where we do not. Both can exist simultaneously and are essential for uncovering deeper layers of truth.[2]

Both/And *and* Either/Or Thinking: When we aim to keep the range of possibilities open in order to navigate complexity, there are times when nuance and paradox must be held together, and others when discernment or decisive action is needed. Maturity lies in knowing the difference.

Commitment to Repair: When we are willing to address ruptures when they occur, seeking support and returning to the conflict to restore trust when it has been strained, relationships grow more resilient and so do we.[3]

Including and Integrating: When we invite others to join us in expanding the conversation, we help weave multiple perspectives into a more comprehensive, integrated experience of a unified whole.[4]

These principles are not merely techniques to master, but ways of being. They are orientations that invite fuller contact with one another and with the dynamic, relational field that exists between us. When we learn to embody the qualities inherent in these principles, dialogue moves beyond communication and becomes a practice of transformation.

OUR WAY BACK TO ONE ANOTHER

I recently had the opportunity to witness these principles come to life in real time, while facilitating a community health initiative to increase access to preventative care for people who have been underserved in my local town. Our group consisted of a diverse mix of clinicians, administrators, and community advocates, each with their own agendas and communication styles. Unsurprisingly, we had hit a wall. Tensions were high, and the room was heavy with frustration. Then Sandy, a local liaison with strong community ties, stood up and spoke.

"I know this might sound like resistance," she said, "but in my community, decisions made too quickly don't land well. If we rush, we might meet the deadline, but we could lose the trust we've only just begun to build."

Her words shifted the energy in the room. Instead of pushing back, the project manager, Brenda, paused and responded with genuine curiosity: "What does trust-building look like where you live?"

The dynamic changed. We stopped pushing for outcomes and started asking better questions. We began hosting listening sessions with community members, making space for stories and nuance. Our original timeline was extended, but the impact became more meaningful when it aligned with the community's actual needs rather than our assumptions about their needs.

That particular exchange became a turning point for the health initiative, not because we found the perfect solution but because we chose to lead from relationship rather than from agenda. This required us to soften societal expectations that speed means efficiency and success means quantity. Instead, over time, we gained presence, responsiveness, and care in shaping the process. And the community felt the difference.

DIALOGUE AS A PROCESS OF BECOMING

When practiced in this way, dialogue is transformed from a method to a way of being. It reveals our relational patterns. Some of us naturally bring structure. Others intuitively hold space. Some lead with action and decisiveness. Others lead with expressiveness and nuance.

These differences mirror the inner polarity we are exploring throughout this book—the dynamic interplay of masculine and feminine energies that live within each of us. One energy moves outward, defining and directing. The other turns inward, receiving and attuning. One asserts; the other listens. Both are essential.

When we favor only one side of this polarity, our conversations become unbalanced. We become combative or compliant, dominating or disengaged. When we learn to integrate both, dialogue becomes an alchemical space where logic meets emotion, discernment is held within tenderness, and structure and flow come into relationship, aligned with what the situation requires.

This is the intelligence of the Communal Heart—a way of being with ourselves and one another that honors difference and invites transformation.

The Communal Heart reminds us that relational wisdom does not arise from mastery, but from our willingness to listen, to be present, and to soften, especially when it's hard. Rather than withdraw when things become difficult, we can expand our tolerance and return to presence. Through this kind of practice, we begin to gently unwind the patterns of polarization that pull us apart, not by forcing agreement or glossing over difference, but by creating the conditions for trust, emergence, and, ultimately, a new kind of culture to take root. In this way, we begin to enact the culture we long to live in, one grounded in presence, shaped by mutuality, and sustained by coherence.

A CULTURE ROOTED IN RELATIONAL WISDOM

The promise of dialogue is not only personal; it is also cultural. In an era when both shouting and silence dominate our public discourse, we are in desperate need of another way. I believe this cultural shift begins with courageous listening and creative communion, as described in these pages. To meet what is required of our time, we must be willing to sit in the fire of difference and discover not enemies or opposition, but mirrors and insight.

This path is not easy. It requires patience, humility, and emotional fortitude. Yet it is both necessary and urgent. For some, dialogue rooted in relational wisdom becomes more than a communication tool; it becomes a sacred practice, fostering deeper connection with others and with the community as a whole. It honors the profound truth that exists between us—a truth that can emerge only when we are fully present with one another, open, and willing to be changed.

In Chapter 9, we will explore what happens when relationships rupture and how the process of repair can bring us even closer, for rupture is also part of the journey. When we meet rupture with presence and curiosity, it can become a doorway to stronger trust, greater intimacy, and the ever-unfolding wisdom of the Communal Heart.

Chapter 9
CRACKS THAT BRING US CLOSER

Conflict is not the end of the relationship;
it is the invitation to deepen it.
—Anonymous

Even with great skill in generative dialogue, periods of disconnection are inevitable. Misunderstandings happen. Needs go unmet. Feelings get hurt. Still, these ruptures are not signs of failure; they show that what we value is at stake. They remind us that we care and that we are, indeed, in relationship. What shapes the outcome is not whether rupture occurs, but how we respond in its aftermath. That response determines whether the relationship frays or finds its way back to wholeness.

I once worked with a couple, Ash and Mallory, who had been together for many years. A single interaction stirred old wounds. Ash felt unseen. Mallory felt blamed. They drifted apart for several days, each unsure how to bridge the growing distance between them. Finally, in a facilitated space, Ash spoke softly: "I didn't know what to say. I got scared and withdrew."

Mallory exhaled. "I just needed to know I still mattered to you."

The repair wasn't polished or even complete, but it was sincere. And in that instant, the hurt between them began to heal.

This is the power of repair. It is the courage to say, "Let's come back." Because it is not perfection that sustains connection but our willingness to return, again and again, to the field of belonging.

THE HIDDEN GIFT OF RUPTURE

Rupture can take many forms. It may be quiet, like a glance that lands the wrong way, or thunderous, like a slammed door. Sometimes, it arrives in an instant, in a dismissal or an overlooked need. Other times, it gathers slowly through prolonged silence, quiet avoidance, or the accumulating weight of tacit disappointment.

Whatever the form, the body knows what the mind may try to deny. Rupture almost always hurts. We brace. We shut down. We defend. Our nervous system registers that a precious connection has been interrupted.

And yet, rupture also carries potential. When we meet it with curiosity rather than avoidance, rupture becomes a threshold. We do not return to how things were, but instead open to more honesty, more completeness, and possibly even more aliveness.

Whether in personal relationships, within communities, or across cultural divides, rupture is part of the path. Just as natural systems periodically break down in order to adapt, reorganize, and evolve, so too do human systems. Our task is to learn how to navigate rupture together and remain open to being transformed by what we discover along the way.

In a culture that tends to equate conflict with failure, we risk missing the invitation that rupture holds. We miss the opportunity to grow, build steadier trust, and cultivate a more resilient form of coherence, one shaped not only by presence but also by our willingness to stay in relationship, especially when it's difficult.

THE ANATOMY OF RUPTURE

While every rupture has its own unique flavor informed by the people, the history, and the time in which it occurs, there are a few common themes that typically show up. One of the biggest ones is unmet need. So often, we assume that those closest to us should know what we're feeling or needing. We expect understanding without actually expressing ourselves clearly. When they don't respond the way we hoped, resentment begins to build.

Then there is emotional overwhelm—situations when stress, fear, or unresolved trauma flood our nervous systems and we are unable to meet what's in front of us. It's not that we don't care about what's going on, but that we've become disconnected from ourselves and, by extension, from the person in front of us. We might shut down, lash out, or go numb, all strategies to do anything but stay present and relational.

Erosion of trust is another slow yet powerful force. It doesn't usually happen in a single instant. Rather, it builds over time through repeated disappointments, unacknowledged hurts, or little betrayals that get swept under the rug. When those minor misattunements accumulate without repair, they leave a residue that can calcify into distance.

Finally, there is cultural friction. Many of us have inherited ways of relating that train us to avoid vulnerability. We're taught to be self-sufficient, to be strong, and to blame or bypass when things get uncomfortable. These patterns live in the collective as much as they live within each of us, forming a kind of feedback loop. This cultural layer may lead us to withdraw or react rather than to stay receptive and engaged with curiosity.

The good news is that when we begin to recognize these patterns with compassion, we open the door to healing and repair. In other words, every rupture, however painful, holds the possibility of greater understanding and renewed connection.

THE PRACTICE OF REPAIR

Because all relationships experience misattunement, what carries us forward is not the absence of rupture but our capacity to return and repair. Repair is the journey of reweaving what has come undone. It is the practice of realigning with the relational field and saying, in essence, "I see where we lost each other, and I want to come back." This practice requires humility and, of course, courage.

A few years ago, I experienced a falling-out with a dear friend. A time of tension spiraled into silence. I waited. She waited. Beneath our withdrawal were unacknowledged fears, strongly held assumptions, and the echo of old stories.

Eventually, I reached out by email. "I regret how that transpired," I wrote. "I value our connection. Can we talk?" She responded quickly by phone. In our conversation, we not only revisited the situation that led to the impasse but also explored the consistent relational patterns we were each carrying.

Repair took time. It took small, sincere gestures to rebuild trust. In the end, the friendship wasn't merely restored. It became more spacious and resilient, allowing us to better understand each other's needs and fears. We now knew we could navigate rupture together.

Repair does not try to erase the wound or pretend it never happened. It transforms the experience into a stronger and more meaningful relationship. Like the Japanese art of kintsugi, where broken pottery is mended with gold, repair doesn't conceal the cracks; it honors them as part of the story.[1] The beauty lies not in perfection but in the resilience that emerges when we choose to return and trust that the relationship can hold what was broken.

PRINCIPLES OF REPAIR

Relational repair is a process. While every situation is different, certain principles can help guide us through the tender terrain of reconnection.

Recognize Rupture: Name the disconnection when it arises rather than ignoring, minimizing, or bypassing it.

Attune to Affect: Listen for what lies beneath the surface, not just the words, but also the emotions, meanings, and stories they carry.

Take Responsibility: Own our part in the rupture with humility, without collapsing into shame or defensiveness.

Make Space for Complexity: Allow room for grief, confusion, silence, and what cannot yet be resolved.

Adjust Behavior: Let the experience change us, not only offering an apology but also showing a sincere willingness to grow.

Rebuild Trust over Time: Allow our actions to consistently affirm our care over time, again and again.

Trust is not built by avoiding pain. It is forged in our courageous willingness to meet pain, our own and that of others, with the curiosity to learn and the tenderness to stay present with ourselves and with one another. There are no guarantees that every attempt at repair will lead to resolution, but each effort strengthens our capacity to listen more deeply, to live more truthfully, and, ultimately, to love more fully. When conflict is met with a commitment to relatedness, it becomes an opportunity for transformation rather than disintegration. Just as our muscles grow stronger through cycles of tension and release, our relationships grow more resilient through the natural rhythms of rupture and repair. Strength comes from practice. From practice comes growth. This capacity to stretch without breaking is what allows the Communal Heart to beat with vitality.

And it is the relational field's flexibility that makes it trustworthy: its ability to include contradiction, to hold paradox, and to recover from missteps. Through this dynamic process, we have an opportunity become more alive and more whole together.

RELATIONAL REPAIR AT SCALE

Learning to repair ruptures in relationships is not only a personal imperative but also a societal one. Just as individuals experience misattunement and disconnection, so too do communities, cultures, and nations. Unacknowledged racial and ethnic harm seeps into the fabric of our culture, leaving wounds that make a collective sense of belonging difficult to realize. Political polarization further fractures our shared reality, as ideology too often replaces genuine understanding and open dialogue. Meanwhile, ecological collapse marks the most profound rupture of all. Our broken relationship with the Earth reveals how far we've strayed from honoring the living systems that sustain us.

To foster cultural repair, we need relational practices that can hold complexity, remain present through discomfort, and weave back the torn threads of trust and belonging. Repair at the societal level cannot be rushed or imposed. It is slow, uncertain work, but history shows that it is possible. Much like interpersonal healing, cultural repair begins when we loosen our grip on stereotypes, harmful cultural representations, and inherited expectations with humility and compassion.

One poignant example of collective repair is South Africa's Truth and Reconciliation Commission (TRC).[2] In the wake of apartheid, a system built on institutionalized racism, violence, and dehumanization, the TRC created a space for both victims and perpetrators to come forward and speak the truth. It was not a traditional courtroom. There were no formal prosecutions or sentences. Instead, it was a space designed for testimony, for public witnessing, and for the acknowledgment of pain that had long been suppressed.

The goal wasn't to erase the past or excuse wrongdoing but to face it squarely and head-on—to name what had been done, grieve it openly, and begin the long, slow process of healing. People told their stories, frequently for the first time, with trembling voices and tear-streaked faces, while others listened in silence, their hearts breaking open in the presence of unfiltered truth.

The process of forgiveness was far from perfect. Not all voices were heard. And certainly, not all wounds were healed. However, it made a profound difference. The TRC marked a cultural shift from retribution to restoration and from denial to recognition. It represented relational courage on a national scale, a public willingness to essentially see, hear, and begin again. In doing so, the TRC became a model for what is possible when a society chooses repair over revenge and dares to bring presence, responsibility, and humanity to the work of reconciliation. It showed that even in the aftermath of profound harm, the act of witnessing together can lay the groundwork for a more truthful and life-affirming future.

As this remarkable historical example demonstrates, authentic repair, whether in our most intimate relationships or across societal divides, requires the vulnerability and sincere willingness to take responsibility, not just once but repeatedly over time.

THE COMMUNAL HEART AS A SOURCE OF RESILIENCE

When rupture is met relationally, a new kind of strength is born. It is not the brittle strength of domination or the ruthless need to win at all costs but the supple strength of resilience that emerges through the ongoing process of knowing and being known. Relational resilience means recognizing that when we stop fearing the rupture and begin trusting the mend, we discover that rupture isn't the end of connection but a necessary part of its evolution.

In a resilient system, difference is held rather than erased. Hurt is acknowledged rather than minimized. Repair is expected rather than avoided. This is the Communal Heart in motion, and its natural rhythm is strengthened with each return to presence, mutuality, and coherence. Most importantly, even when we lose the thread, the field remains. It waits for us. It welcomes us back. In that return, repair becomes the path home, not to how things once were, but to who we are becoming, together.

As we move to Part IV to explore healing the communal divide among us, we carry forward the lessons of repair. Integration often involves rupture, both within us and between one another. To live from the Communal Heart is to trust in the capacity of relationship to hold complexity and to understand healing as an ongoing, unfolding process rather than a fixed destination. Even when something feels broken, we are rarely beyond repair.

This is the promise of dialogue. This is the practice of love.

An Invitation to Practice the Communal Heart in Dialogue

Conversations can become more than an exchange of words; they can become a living expression of the relational field. The Communal Heart is present when we speak from embodied experience—sensing, feeling, and thinking—rather than relying on habitual reactions or rehearsed opinions. As you move forward, listen with the intention to understand, not merely agree or disagree. When differences arise, hold space for them with patience and curiosity without needing to resolve them right away.

Check-In: Are You in Relational Presence?

Before or during a conversation, ask yourself the following:

- Am I grounding in trust or trying to control the outcome?
- Am I making space for emergence or rushing to conclusions?
- Am I speaking from a place of coherence or reacting from fear, defensiveness, or impatience?

Recognizing these patterns shifts us from habitual interaction to relational wisdom. This is the hallmark of the paradoxical nature of change.[1]

Part IV

RETURNING TO THE WORLD WE SHARE

Chapter 10

A REUNION WE LONG FOR

Wholeness is not achieved by cutting off a portion of one's being, but by integration of the contraries.

—Carl Jung

We have arrived at the heart of our journey, where healing within, between, and among us begins to converge. Up to this point, we've explored how to heal our inner world and repair our relationships with others. Now, we widen the lens to consider how we begin to heal the fundamental rupture running through modern culture itself.

At the center of this cultural divide lies a long-standing rift between the masculine and the feminine. As explored in earlier chapters, this fracture is not simply about gender. It reflects the archetypal and energetic currents that move through us and reveals a perceptual imbalance woven into the fabric of modern consciousness. Our dominant culture has come to privilege an abstract, instrumental, and goal-driven mode of attention expressed by the left hemisphere while undervaluing a relational, embodied, and context-sensitive mode of attention more fully expressed through the right hemisphere. This neglected way of knowing has often been culturally associated with the feminine, further amplifying the imbalance in how we perceive and relate to the world.

For too long, this natural polarity has been cast as strict opposites pitted against each other rather than honored as complementary movements in the shared dance of life. This false separation has shaped our social institutions, personal relationships, and even our sense of self, reinforcing patterns of fragmentation and disconnection.

But what if this natural polarity, arising from biological conditions, expressed through attentional and perceptual tendencies, and reinforced through culture, was not meant to be held apart but to be reunited? What if this is the deeper invitation of our time? I believe it is.

Healing the cultural rift between the masculine and feminine begins within ourselves, where it first takes shape. But this does not require sameness, nor does it erase difference. Instead, it invites us into relationship. It asks that we honor what each energy brings, allowing these distinct ways of attending to life to meet, inform, and temper each other. This is the integration now being called forth: a weaving of these gifts into wholeness within ourselves, between us, and across the culture we share.

At their best, these archetypal energies serve life. The masculine offers focus, discernment, and the capacity for responsible action. The feminine offers presence, attunement, and the ability to hold what is emerging. Together, they form a relational field capable of coherence.

However, when these energies become distorted and their relationship is lost—when the masculine overasserts or imposes, or when the feminine withdraws or collapses—the relational field begins to fray. Disconnection takes hold, not only between individuals but also within the very patterns of thought, feeling, and action that shape our shared world. Culture, in turn, becomes a mirror and amplifier of this inner division.

The way forward is not to reverse the imbalance by placing women solely in charge of public life, as this would simply invert rather than heal the split. Nor is it to flatten difference, which would diminish the creative potential that difference makes possible. Healing this divide in modern culture requires discernment, patience, and sustained effort. It asks us to honor the polarity of the masculine and the feminine as a vital, generative tension, one that must be consciously held, integrated, and tended with care.

This work draws us into the slow, creative process of integration, calling us into coherence through the cultivation of a balanced attention that supports an integrated way of attending to life. Through this kind of communion, a relational field emerges, supple enough to hold our differences and strong enough to grow through them. In its deepest sense, this path leads us into the heart of collective belonging, where the sacred dance between the masculine and feminine becomes a living expression of wholeness itself.

A PARTNERSHIP CREATED FOR LIFE

To bring this possibility of integration into view, I offer a story. It echoes a classic parable, a reimagining of *The Master and His*

Emissary, which Iain McGilchrist uses to illustrate the perceptual divide at the core of modern Western life.[1] In McGilchrist's version, the emissary, meant to serve the master, usurps the master's role, seizes control, and eventually severs the kingdom from the wisdom it once relied upon.

In the version that follows, I bring a relational lens to the tale. This story centers on the dynamic interplay between the masculine and the feminine. Rather than simply portraying inversion, in which the emissary forgets his place, this retelling invites us to consider the possibility of healing through integration. It illuminates a sacred partnership in which masculine action remains connected to feminine wisdom, and where presence and purpose move together, in partnership with life.

In a thriving kingdom, there once was a wise and intuitive Queen who reigned, not through force or decree, but through relational attunement. She governed by sensing into the whole, feeling subtle shifts in the collective field, and perceiving the unseen threads that knitted all things together, including the land to which she and her people belonged. Her power was quiet but profound, rooted in presence and in the intimate knowing of what was needed before it was even spoken.

It soon became clear that her awareness longed for form as she saw her kingdom ready to take shape. So she chose a Knight who could translate her vision with integrity and responsible action in service of the greater good. Together, they cultivated a natural rhythm. The Queen perceived the whole picture, while the Knight focused on the details.

The Queen held space with reverence, and the Knight moved forward with courage. In this sacred alliance, perception and action were woven into a single fabric of living intelligence. The kingdom flourished, and life cohered, until the Knight became captivated by the particulars.

Gradually, almost imperceptibly, the Knight began to forget to consult with his Queen. He started to mistake agency for meaning and progress for wisdom. Listening gave way to striving, and responsiveness gave way to control. Slowly and consistently, the rhythm between them dissolved, and the kingdom began to change.

Although the kingdom became more efficient and undoubtedly more productive, it also began to lose its soul. The once-felt sense of unity unraveled into separation. What had previously moved in harmony now moved in fragments, leaving the kingdom less cohesive and its inhabitants increasingly uneasy.

As we already know, this is not only a metaphor; it is also a pattern we can recognize in our lives and our modern culture. We see it whenever action outpaces attunement or when the drive to produce eclipses the wisdom of presence.

REMEMBERING THE QUEEN

My friend Jack, a former environmental science teacher, offers a living example of this dynamic. After many years in the classroom, he found himself burned out. His students, once curious about the natural world, had become more focused on grades than on learning for its own sake. Rather than continue participating in a system driven more by metrics than meaning, Jack chose a different path. He left teaching in search of what had first drawn him to environmental science. With no clear plan, only a desire to reconnect with what felt fulfilling, he moved from the suburbs of the Bay Area to the coast of central California, returning to a place he had once considered home.

He took a significant financial risk and purchased an undeveloped piece of land. In the beginning, he camped there for weeks at a time, sleeping outdoors beneath the stars and orienting himself to the natural environment. He paid attention to the wind, the light, and the movement of birds overhead. He spent long hours with his hands in the soil, learning its texture and moisture content. Soon, a rhythm emerged. The land began to offer guidance, not through ideas but through ongoing contact. Jack responded by listening. Slowly, he began to build a homestead, first with a small one-room house and then a garden. There was no rush. Each step arose from an unfolding conversation he was having with the land, shaped by season, weather, and necessity.

Jack started sharing his homestead with others. He invited friends and neighbors to walk on the property, plant gardens, and gather around a fire in the evenings. People cooked meals, talked about what was working and what wasn't, and exchanged experiences of life on the coast. Over time, a steady presence began to form. Trustworthy intimacy took root among them in their relationships, grounded in shared presence, mutual respect, and care for one another and for the place where they all felt they belonged.

Eventually, others in the area noticed. A few local articles were written about what Jack had initiated. Then came invitations to speak about his experiences, requests to formalize what he was doing, and questions about how it might be scaled or replicated. Jack said yes, as so many of us would. He wanted to make a difference in a world that seems to have lost its way.

Before long, his attention shifted. He spent more time traveling than tending, more time explaining than listening. Interviews, panels, and proposals replaced mornings on the land. While his days grew full, they were no longer fulfilling. Soon, he noticed an old ache had returned. He had moved from stewarding relationships to managing outcomes. The intimacy that had once been at the heart of his daily interactions—the sacred act of listening and then responding—was slowly contracting. In a language he would later recognize, Jack had forgotten his Queen.

Stepping back was not an easy choice. It meant turning away from public recognition and the promise of influence and realigning with his own values and the rhythms of nature itself. In time, he let go of the projects and the public-facing role and returned to the land. I remember him describing one afternoon when he lay in the tall grass near his little house: "I needed to be in touch with this place again," he said with humility. Once he did, he settled in place. He reconnected with the source that had first drawn him to the coast, as a felt sense of being at home.

Jack was remembering his Queen, the part of him that knows how to attend and, more importantly, how to trust what arises in stillness. In this reunion, he realized that his initial offering was never meant to be an outcomes-driven model but rather a way of being, shared with those who wished to cultivate a presence grounded in reverence for the life unfolding all around them.

MATURITY AS INTEGRATION MADE VISIBLE

Jack's story reflects the broader story of our modern culture. We live in a world shaped by Knights who have forgotten their Queens. We are praised for productivity, not presence. We are taught to fix rather than to feel. We rush into action, often without pausing to consider what our actions are truly in service of.

This imbalance reveals itself in countless ways. In workplaces, the relentless pursuit of outcomes often eclipses the dignity and well-being of those involved. In leadership, dominance is too often valued over the gifts of receptivity. In institutions and politics, complexity is flattened into slogans, and power is wielded to maintain control.

However, the Communal Heart calls us to follow another path. It invites us into a rhythm of mutuality between doing and being, between the masculine and the feminine, and into the wisdom that emerges through integration.

To live this balance is to mature, not necessarily in the superficial sense of age, achievement, or social status, but in our capacity to hold the tension of opposites with grace. A mature person can feel deeply and still act with discernment. They can speak what they currently believe to be true without shutting others down. They can stay open to another's perspective without losing their own. And they can discern without imposing and receive without collapsing into passivity.

In other words, maturity is the art of knowing when to step in and when to hold back. It is the capacity to be both expansive and clear, soft and strong, and to hold the tension of polarity without rushing to resolve it. Maturity invites us to resist the pull of old patterns and rigid roles and instead attune to what life is truly asking for in each moment. Most of all, maturity is the capacity to stay present amid complexity—to move with the energy the circumstances require, not from habit or fear but from presence and a fuller sense of relationship with ourselves, one another, and the world around us.

I once worked with a family consisting of a mother, father, and teenage son. The relationship between father and son had grown tense, marked by arguments, long silences, and the pain of mutual misunderstanding. As in many strained relationships between parents and children, they were caught in a pattern where neither felt fully seen or heard by the other.

The mother had long approached parenting through relational attunement. She naturally embodied receptivity, empathizing with her son's inner world and holding space for his feelings without rushing to fix them. She reflected his internal experience back to him, helping him understand himself and laying the foundation for basic trust and self-awareness.[2]

The father, on the other hand, was more action-oriented. He believed in preparing his son for the world beyond their familial environment, in setting clear expectations and firm boundaries. His role had always centered on helping his son meet reality with analytic precision and personal agency. But in this particular impasse, his usual tools weren't working. The more he pushed, the more his son pulled away. How they were relating needed to change. To his credit, the father began choosing a different path.

In a facilitated session during a tense exchange that could have easily followed a familiar script of punishment, defensiveness, or emotional withdrawal, the father paused to reflect on his wife's strengths. Instead of reacting, he took time to reflect, not only on his son's behavior but also on his own emotional reactivity. He recognized that his instinct to assert authority would only widen the gap. Rather than that, he slowed down to listen to himself, to his son, and to what the situation was asking of him.

Then he spoke from presence. He acknowledged the hurt that had arisen within him and between them without shaming his son or blaming himself. He described the distance that had formed and invited his son into a space of honest repair. There was no power play, just fairness and care held together. His masculine capacity for discernment, his ability to see the details clearly and name what was true for him, was softened and deepened by a feminine quality of receptivity, relational attunement, and the willingness to feel into his son's pain. As a result, he neither tried to control his son's behavior nor collapsed in self-pity. Instead, he stayed present, open, and steady.

Gradually, the dynamic between his son and him began to shift. His son didn't just hear his father's words; he felt the integrity behind them, too. That conversation became a turning point. Their relationship didn't merely "go back to normal." It deepened. It became more honest and sincere.

Their experience illustrates the power of mature responsiveness as a way of being that arises when we bring the best of the masculine and best of the feminine into relationship, allowing discernment, compassion, fairness, and care to work together in service of life.

This story could have unfolded differently, of course. There are many situations in which a mother may need to remember the discernment and fairness her partner brings, especially when empathy alone isn't enough. The point is not to assign fixed roles or judge one orientation over the other but to recognize how these qualities live in all of us and can be called forth as needed.

COLLABORATIVE LEADERSHIP

When we begin to value the masculine and feminine energies within ourselves, we come to value them more fully in our shared culture. Nowhere is this more consequential than in leadership. Mature leaders neither rush impulsively into solutions nor withdraw into avoidance. They resist the pull of urgency that demands immediate answers and instead choose to slow down. They pause. They listen, not only to what is being said, but also to the emotional undertones and unspoken tensions beneath the words. Attuned to the relational field, they sense what is present, what is emerging, and what is being asked for.

Rather than reacting from habit or fear, they respond from a felt sense of relatedness. While attending to the particulars of a situation, mature leaders also hold the wider context—the unseen dynamics, the history, and the potential futures shaping the moment. Because their actions are rooted in presence, they understand that sustainable change arises from aligning our inner and outer worlds and from coherence with the subtler currents moving through our shared reality.

To lead from balanced attention and integrated engagement is to return to the Queen and the Knight within, ensuring that movement emerges from meaning and that action remains in service to life. When the inner Queen, receptive and attuned, guides the Knight, focused and directed, leadership becomes less a struggle for power and more a practice of stewardship. As we will explore later in the book, when this inner balance is extended into partnership with others, leadership itself becomes a shared field. It becomes a collaborative endeavor held by many rather than a burden carried by one. This is the kind of leadership that our times urgently need, one capable of meeting the metacrisis with wisdom.

LOVE AS AN ATTRACTOR

The reunion of the Queen and her Knight is not an abstract theory. We can feel it in our bodies. I experience it most clearly during long-distance runs when my breath falls into cadence with my steps, and my thoughts gradually settle into the rhythm of presence. The noise of striving recedes, and a subtler intelligence takes the lead. As my awareness widens, my body remembers its place in the greater pattern of belonging. I am no longer trying to control the moment. I am being *moved* by it.

And so, I run, not only for exercise, but also to return to the field where everything belongs, not because I have earned it, but because I have come back into a natural rhythm with life.

From this lived rhythm, we begin to glimpse what is possible when the masculine and feminine reunite and integrate. In Chapter 11, we will explore how this reunion opens a threshold to the vital relational energy of love. This is not love in the narrow sense of personal emotion or romantic attachment, though it may include both. Rather, it is love as a fractal of coherence, a living relational field that carries the same pattern across every scale. It is born of balanced attention, sustained through relationship, and animated by the transforming currents that flow between people and the natural world.

This is our work now: to co-create a world shaped by love as a way of being, where the process of knowing and being known remains alive between us. Love, in this fuller sense, is the pulse of the Communal Heart, the field of belonging that, when remembered, has the power to mend what has long been fractured and to guide us toward a more whole, humane, and connected future.

Chapter 11
THE THIRD WAY OPENS A NEW PATH

Out beyond ideas of wrongdoing and rightdoing,
there is a field. I'll meet you there.
—Rumi

We have all experienced moments when we feel caught between two opposing pulls. Perhaps it's the tension between speaking up and keeping the peace, or the draw between staying home to read a good book and going out dancing with close friends. Or, on a lighter note, it might be the simple choice between vanilla and chocolate ice cream. Such moments can leave us feeling as though we must choose sides, as if honoring one means abandoning the other.

We live in a world that so easily pulls us into oppositional thinking. From an early age, we're taught to divide reality into fixed categories: right or left, open or closed, emotion or reason. These binaries shape not only our politics and institutions, but also our inner lives. For example, just as voters feel pressed to distill their complex political leanings into rigid labels of "blue" or "red," other aspects of identity and experience are often reduced to binary choices, narrowing a wide field of expression into fixed ideas.

While categorization can simplify complexity and make understanding possible, experience shows that life rarely fits neatly into black-and-white boxes. Life is a process, a living field of relationships—messy, dynamic, and rich with nuance. When we remain trapped in either/or thinking, we limit ourselves to false choices and reactive postures. We cling to one side of a polarity and reject the other, often without noticing the cost. As a result, we miss the deeper wisdom available to us, the kind of wisdom that emerges only in the tension between apparent opposites.

This chapter invites us to engage with presumed binaries, not as a compromise or a watered-down middle ground, but as a fuller integration that both transcends and includes polarity. Many spiritual traditions call this integrative process the reconciling force, the creative energy that arises when we hold opposing truths. Rather than flattening differences, this force honors them, bringing forth something new from the tension between them, something more alive and complete than either could offer alone.

In everyday life, the reconciling force is profoundly consequential. It appears in the conversations we dare remain in and the relationships we choose to repair rather than abandon. Through this force, we move from fragmentation toward wholeness.

THE LAW OF THREE IN EVERYDAY LIFE

You likely experienced this integrative force in your own life, perhaps without realizing it had a name—those moments when a new possibility emerges from the generous act of holding tension rather than rushing to resolve it.

Imagine a moment of conflict with someone you love. Part of you wants to lean in, to listen and understand. That is the initiating force.[1] Another part of you wants to step back, to resist, protect, or even shut down. This is the denying force. Both impulses are real and valid, yet they seem to cancel each other out, leaving you stuck in inner conflict.

Then, the unexpected occurs. Maybe you pause and take a breath. Maybe you go for a walk, cook a meal, or sleep on it. In that space between openness and withdrawal, between context and concern, a new path appears. The Queen and her Knight reunite, and your perspective shifts. You begin to see your loved one's pain, or you feel your own fear loosen. You're no longer trapped between yes and no. Instead, a new Gestalt forms, revealing a way forward that wasn't visible before. That is the reconciling force.[2]

This path forward is not a compromise. You're not giving up or giving in. Instead, you're honoring both sides of the tension and allowing a mature response born from relational wisdom to emerge, one that both transcends and includes the polarities at play. This is the essence of what some spiritual traditions call the Law of Three.[3]

We see this principle in action everywhere:

A seed (initiating) meets the density of soil (denying), yet nothing grows without sun and water (reconciling).

We inhale (gathering) and we exhale (release), but the pause between (integrating) is the sacred space of integration that makes breathing conscious, nourishing, and complete.

A father (who provides discipline) and a mother (who gives empathy) struggle to find common ground until a third way to parent their child appears, an approach that blends fairness with care, holding both nurture and structure, presence and boundary.

The Law of Three reminds us that conflict is not always a problem to fix. Sometimes, it is a portal instead. When we can stay with the tension without collapsing into either extreme, we open space for a new intelligence to arise.

RELATIONAL INTELLIGENCE IN ACTION

I have witnessed the pull of polarity play out with many couples over the years. One partner may crave spontaneity, while the other longs for predictability and routine. These are natural preferences, but when they become rigid positions, partners tend to polarize around them. As tension escalates, their connection begins to fray. Each person feels unseen or unmet, and, in an effort to protect themselves, retreats further into their stance.

Yet I've also witnessed a remarkable shift occur when both partners remain present without rushing to resolve the conflict or withdrawing from it. In those moments, the tension itself becomes a doorway. What emerges is not a watered-down compromise, but a deeper, more generative way of being together. A new dynamic takes shape, one that honors both needs without collapsing into either. In this space, each partner is invited to become more fully themselves, not in opposition to the relationship, but *through* it. The very tension that once threatened their bond becomes the force that strengthens it.

A few years ago, I worked with a couple named Aracelli and Omar. Both were thoughtful, attentive, and very committed to their marriage, but their approaches to conflict couldn't have been more different. Aracelli was a quick problem-solver. She was efficient, pragmatic, and eager to move things forward. Omar, by contrast, tended to absorb emotional tension. He often mediated, deflected, or smoothed over discomfort to maintain harmony between them.

One evening, they found themselves up against a familiar impasse. Aracelli wanted to make a significant financial decision involving their shared savings. Omar wasn't necessarily opposed to the idea itself, but the speed at which it was occurring unsettled him. Aracelli's urgency reminded him of his childhood, where sudden decisions and instability often went hand in hand.

But this time, Omar chose a different response. Instead of deflecting or accommodating too quickly, he paused. He turned inward. He checked in with his body and emotions, noticing a tightness in his throat and a knot in his stomach. He realized he wasn't afraid of Aracelli. He was afraid of his own silence, a silence that had so often swallowed his needs. Rather than pushing his discomfort aside, he stayed with it. He breathed. He let himself feel what was emerging without rushing to fix it or explain it away. In that slowing down, he created space, not just for himself, but for Aracelli's experience as well.

Sensing his shift, Aracelli also slowed down. She stopped pressing for answers and began to reflect, not only on the financial decision at hand, but also on how her urgency might be affecting him. She started to understand that Omar's need for pacing and safety wasn't resistance but arose from the wisdom of his nervous system and lived experience.

They agreed to revisit the decision at another time. When they eventually did, the conversation unfolded with tenderness and mutual regard. Together, they arrived at a path forward that honored both of their needs—financial prudence and relational safety. What emerged was a new possibility that both transcended and included their individual experiences.

This is the reconciling force in motion. It doesn't flatten the difference. It moves through difference. It doesn't settle for either/or. It finds a third way, not as a compromise, but as co-creation.

HEALING THE DIVIDE OF MODERN LIFE

We are being asked to address a similar tension on a cultural scale. Modernity brought forth systems based on dominance hierarchy, scientific rationalism, and individual achievement, structures that fueled immense progress but at the expense of relational depth and collective care. In response, postmodernity, through the civil rights movement, women's liberation, justice reform, and environmentalism, rose to challenge those systems, exposing hidden power dynamics, questioning objectivity, and amplifying the voices long left out. In its critique, however, it also flattened difference and left a vacuum that too easily slid into nihilism.

Now, we stand at a new threshold.[4] The pendulum is swinging, and we are being pulled between intensifying poles—authoritarianism and anarchy, fact and counterfactual, nationalism and globalization. The fragmentation is palpable, not only in our politics and institutions but also in our psyches and relationships.

We face an urgent task. We must learn to remain present with the cultural tension long enough for a reconciling force to emerge, one that doesn't collapse into the old binaries but carries forward the best of both modernity and postmodernity into a generative and new relational way of being. We begin this work close to home, within our intimate relationships and in the shared cultural story we are here to reimagine together. At the heart of this integrative path, what I have been calling the Communal Heart, lies a facet of relational intelligence that many mothers and caregivers have long modeled.[5]

THE GROUND OF BELONGING

Despite the profound challenges that it entails, parenthood offers a direct connection to a way of being that prioritizes something greater than the self. Nowhere is this more evident than in a healthy relationship between a mother and her infant.[6] While undoubtedly imperfect, their bond reflects a state of loving interconnectedness that is not earned but given. In this sense, the love between mother and child is a foundational pattern of universal love that emerges from the ground of belonging and scales outward into the wider world we all share.

Much like many human mothers, this ground of belonging is marked by patience and responsiveness. It does not impose or demand. It waits. It offers a relational space into which we are invited, uncoerced, to awaken. Within this space of mutual attunement lies the quiet wisdom of restraint, a deep trust in the unfolding of life rather than a need to manage it.

When we begin to recognize that this ground of belonging needs us just as much as we need it, our core understandings of the world shift. We move from passive recipients of life to active participants in its beauty. We begin to fall in love with reality again—to cherish it not as a resource to be used but as a sacred, living presence to be tended. Where there is sacredness, there is intimacy. Where there is intimacy, there is allurement, reverence, and perhaps most importantly, a bidirectional flow of devotion.[7]

This dimension of relational intelligence invites us, as a modern culture, into deeper alignment with life. It calls us to shift from patterns of dominance to practices of communion. For too long, our collective orientation has been shaped by habits of narrow, abstract attention and largely one-way relating, patterns that have profoundly influenced many Western institutions and ways of organizing life. While differentiation and focused attention continue to serve essential functions, our times are asking more of us. They call for a fuller, more balanced, and integrated way of attending, alongside a more embodied, responsive way of engaging—a way of being that honors the living field of connection in which we are already embedded.

LOVE AS THE RECONCILING FORCE

At the heart of this co-creative dynamic is love, not as a fleeting sentiment but as a relational force capable of holding the generative tension between the archetypal energies of chaos and order, often associated with the feminine and masculine, without collapsing into either.[8] Like broad and narrow attention, chaos and order reflect complementary energies whose dynamic interplay mirrors the right hemisphere's openness to possibility and context and the left hemisphere's capacity to differentiate and give form. Together, they give rise to our inner lives, our outer environment, and our shared culture.

Though easily misunderstood, chaos here refers not to disorder, but to the energy of possibility. Chaos invites creativity and emergence. Order brings direction and structure. One leans toward expansion, the other toward stability. With relational wisdom, order becomes a threshold through which chaos can be meaningfully expressed. Without order, chaos dissolves into dispersion. Without chaos, order turns rigid and lifeless. Yet together, chaos and order create the generative tension through which life unfolds and thrives.

It is in the dance between these two—the open palm of chaos and the steady grasp of order, or the Queen and her Knight—that we learn how to relate, create, and become. These two fundamental energies, distinct yet inseparable, weave the very fabric of reality itself. For without separation, there can be no true reunion; without the other, there can be no falling in love.

Love may be at the heart of our collective healing. Even under the lens of postmodern critique, modernity continues to condition us. We relate through utility, treating people, systems, and even ourselves as means to an end. The Communal Heart offers a different orientation. It reminds us that relationship is not a byproduct of life but its very purpose.

When we align ourselves with the field of relationality—the field of love—we begin to move from competition to communion. We shift from separation to solidarity and from fragmentation to wholeness. This reorientation does not happen all at once. It unfolds gradually through presence, restraint, and the small but consequential acts of continuing to show up for ourselves, for one another, and for the sacred space between and beyond us. In time, through our shared work, culture responds in kind.

In Chapter 12, we will explore the Communal Heart as both a path and a place, a living journey and an emergent destination. It is a call to return, not to where we began, but to where we belong in rhythm, in relationship, and in love.

Chapter 12

THE DYNAMIC REALITY OF BELONGING

Reality is not something you inhabit or perceive;
it's something you participate in co-creating.
—Hanzi Freinacht

When we begin to live from the field of love, a different world comes into view. We stop seeing life as a string of isolated events and begin to recognize it as a vast, dynamic web of interdependent connections. Relationships no longer appear as mere transactions but as threads in a larger tapestry of meaning, and we begin to understand that we live in a participatory universe, one in which our presence, our choices, and our ways of relating shape what we are part of, even as it shapes us.

Relational intelligence, at its core, is not only about empathy or attunement but also about recognizing patterns across time and scale. It involves the ability to notice what is recurring and what is trying to emerge, from the rhythm of our breath to the tone of a conversation, from the dynamics of a family system to the direction of a culture. When we learn to see these relational patterns with clarity and compassion, we begin to respond in ways that align with life rather than resist or override it.

I was reminded of this recently while walking through a redwood forest after facilitating a particularly intense group retreat. Although the retreat had ended, my body still carried the remnants of residual tension—a tight jaw, shallow breath, and a sense of unresolved conflict. As I walked, I intentionally slowed and dropped into my senses, smelling the soil and bark, hearing the hush beneath the towering canopy, and seeing the tender green of new growth nestled beside ancient trunks. Once I settled in place, I remembered that these trees are not separate from one another. They are linked by an underground network of mycelium, a living web through which they share nutrients, caretaking, and even warning signals. What appears aboveground to be individual is, indeed, sustained by relationships.[1]

So it is with us, too. Belonging, like a forest, is not a fixed or static condition. It is a dynamic, living pattern of relationships that we can feel, practice, and restore. It asks that we stay in touch with the flow of life moving through us and around us, and that we remember that even when we feel isolated, we are still part of something larger. Healing across personal, relational, and cultural domains begins when we remember this shared existential truth.

FRACTALS OF CONNECTION

In mathematics, a fractal is a recursive pattern that repeats itself at every scale. We see it in nature, in seashells, in leaf veins, and in river deltas. Each part reflects the whole, whether we look closely or from a distance.

Relational life is fractal, too. The presence we bring to any particular moment extends beyond it. How we tend to a single conversation—how we listen, how we respond, how we stay present—shapes not only that exchange but also the emotional tone of our relationships, the culture of our families, and even the values embedded in our communities and institutions. This is why the Communal Heart is not just an idea or a poetic metaphor; it is also a real, lived pattern, a fractal of careful attunement and relational coherence that shows up within, between, and among us. It lives in the micro-interactions, such as pausing before reacting, holding another's gaze with presence, and offering our attention as a gift. These small gestures of presence and reciprocity are not, in fact, small. They are seeds that grow, altering the larger patterns we inhabit. In this way, they become the roots of cultural transformation.

One evening, I sat between my sons on a park bench as we watched the sunset. We didn't say much, but the silence between us was full, imbued with mutual recognition and gentle love. Although nothing dramatic happened, everything felt right. And that sense of coherence didn't end there. It stayed with me long afterward, influencing how I showed up for others in the days that followed. I was calmer, more grounded, and more attuned. A simple experience of relational presence became a source of strength and clarity for me. Love had moved subtly but impactfully through us, and I extended it outward even further. This same dynamic unfolds at scale.

Let's reflect again on the Truth and Reconciliation Commission in postapartheid South Africa.[2] Nelson Mandela's leadership was not only political, but also deeply relational. After his decades of imprisonment, his presence was grounded in forgiveness, dignity, and an unwavering commitment to healing, and he guided public policy and stirred the nation's imagination. His capacity to hold pain without perpetuating harm became a cultural template. It became a fractal pattern of relational wisdom that radiated outward, opening the way for a different kind of future.

This is the power of the Communal Heart. It is not abstract but embodied. It lives in the choices we make; in the small, sacred spaces where balanced attention meets the actuality of our lives; and in the larger field of possibility where those choices become a source of life-affirming inspiration for all they touch.

FROM FIGURE TO FIELD

Because modern life conditions us to focus narrowly, we're trained to zero in on the figure, the thing that stands out and grabs our attention. Yet we now know that meaning doesn't arise from the figure alone. It emerges from the background, the wider field in which everything is held. A cup on a desk, for example, carries one meaning in a cozy living room and an entirely different one in a stark hospital corridor. Context shapes our experience. The field holds everything that was, is, and will become.

However, most of our modern systems routinely disregard this contextual awareness. They fragment knowledge into isolated data points, severing meaning from relationship. In doing so, they ignore the deeper truth that we are never separate from the field; we are shaped by it, and we shape it in return.

To live from the Communal Heart is to reclaim contextual awareness by expanding our perceptual field to include not only what is in front of us, but also the often invisible threads that connect us to everything else. This shift from figure to field is not merely cognitive. It transforms how we breathe, how we make decisions, and how we care for ourselves, one another, and the natural systems we are part of.

THE LIVING PATTERN OF LOVE

To embody relationality is to know, deep in our bones, that we are part of a larger, ever-evolving whole. Each breath connects us to the universe. Each word we speak enters a shared field of meaning. Even our silences carry possibility, inviting something profound and unspoken to emerge.

Living from the Communal Heart allows us to loosen our grip on rigid identities, such as self versus other, inner versus outer, masculine versus feminine, and move instead with the flow of life. When we do, we shift from needing control to allowing attunement. We begin by navigating without forcing outcomes, by listening for what the moment is asking of us and responding accordingly.

The love we have been cultivating along this path is not a romantic ideal, but the deeper, subtler current that runs through all of reality. Love is the ultimate fractal. It repeats its pattern across scales, in the steady process of knowing and being known, of seeing and being seen, of attuning across difference without collapsing into sameness. Love is a relational pattern.

I once went backpacking into the Sierra Nevada mountains of Northern California with a few close friends. The journey was strenuous, with steep trails, thin air, and aching muscles, but as we climbed, our attention broadened. We experienced an opening. The higher we went, the quieter and more reverent we became, as if the mountain itself was inviting us into another way of being.

One morning, we rose before sunrise to begin a silent ascent to a nearby peak. Frost crunched beneath our boots, our breath visible in the cold dawn air. Just as we reached the summit, the first rays of sunlight brushed the treetops in the distance. We stood in stillness. Few words were spoken. We simply rested in presence. The land, the sky, our cadence—everything in communion—held together by something larger than ourselves.

I remember placing my hand on a granite boulder, still cool from the night. It grounded me. There was no separation, only a sense of intimate belonging between stone and skin, self and surroundings. As I looked out across the ridgelines, their fractal beauty mirrored the delicate patterns of care we had shared throughout the trip, the small gestures of offering water or slowing our pace to wait for a friend. Love wasn't talked about; it was the field we shared.

That day, I came to understand what I had only sensed before. Love is not merely an emotion, but an energetic pattern. It is a generative current that animates the world. It moves through the way we walk, speak, and listen. It lives in our gestures, our timing, and our tone. Every action shapes the relational field we are a part of, even as it shapes us in return.

When we live from this pattern—when we choose to listen, to stay, and to attune—we become stewards of coherence and midwives of connection in a world that so often forgets how to belong. Life becomes more than a series of tasks or destinations. It becomes relational, alive, and, yes, wise. In this remembering, we realize *we belong to this world*. This is how the Communal Heart beats through us and among us for the healing of the planet as a whole.

LOVE UNFOLDING

The Communal Heart is an invitation to participate more fully in life itself. To live this way is to remember that every moment holds creative potential. Every act, however small, contributes to the larger pattern. Every relationship becomes a portal into the sacredness of reality.

When we begin to experience the fractal nature of being, where each part reflects the whole and the whole lives within every part, we stop waiting for transformation to come from elsewhere. Instead, we realize that we are the transformation. We become the ones who tend the field. We cultivate coherence through the ongoing courage to love, even when it is difficult, even when it is uncertain, even when nothing seems to change.

In Part V, we will explore more closely what this kind of love looks like at scale—how our relationships, communities, and even social systems can reflect this more resonant way of being. Not as an abstract ideal but as a living practice, a way of showing up that restores trust, centers in relationship, and reclaims love as the ground of belonging. Many of us have already committed to living in this way. It doesn't require perfection or grand gestures, only that we begin right where we are, with each breath, each step, each honest question, and each tender pause.

An Invitation to Practice the Communal Heart as an Internal Compass

To live from the Communal Heart is to recognize when we are moving in and out of alignment with the larger relational field, all while making minor course corrections along the way. Remember, it is not a destination but a path of refined attunement.

Check-In: Are You Living from the Communal Heart?

Pause and reflect:

- When did I feel most aligned today—open, present, relationally attuned?
- When did I feel disconnected—rushed, reactive, closed off?
- What slight shift can I make to move toward more presence and trust right now?

Even a conscious breath, a moment of deep listening, or a choice to trust emergence can bring us back into coherence with life itself.

Part V

TOWARD A RELATIONAL FUTURE

Chapter 13
CIRCLES OF RENEWAL

Never doubt that a small group of thoughtful,
committed citizens can change the world;
indeed, it's the only thing that ever has.
—Margaret Mead

Culture rarely transforms solely through grand declarations or sweeping revolutions. Real transformation begins in intimate spaces where people gather with sincerity to live differently. Like a rhizomatic network that spreads nonhierarchically and in multiple directions at once, small community circles quietly regenerate the cultural soil.[1] In these spaces, the seeds of change are being sown through simple, courageous acts of showing up again and again.

Whether called wisdom circles, support pods, learning communities, or sacred councils, these relational spaces are shaped by genuine dialogue and shared intention. As these islands of coherence connect through reciprocal trust and the steady cultivation of relational depth, they offer refuge, not by retreating from reality, but by engaging with it differently. They start with presence, deepen into a commitment to mutual growth, and culminate in a willingness to make sense together. What emerges is a network of relational intelligence capable of carrying coherence across wider systems.[2]

In 2023, during the waning months of the global pandemic, many of us felt disoriented and bereft of the stability we had come to rely on. I found myself thinking of my friend Jack and the way he had re-centered himself by connecting with his small group of neighbors. Inspired by him and concerned that truth itself was becoming increasingly uncertain in a world losing its shared sense of reality, I invited a small group of friends online to stay connected through genuine conversation. There was no plan, only to stay grounded in what we knew to be real. Week after week, we gathered, and over time, an extraordinary process began to unfold. The insights that arose between us were wiser, more nuanced, and more alive than any of us could have arrived at on our own.

From this humble beginning, the international community of Wisdom Exchange was born, not so much an organization as a relational container of trust.[3] We discovered that nourishing connections doesn't require ideology. It requires relational intimacy, where small groups of three to seven share tenderness and vulnerability safely.[4]

SMALL, INTERCONNECTED ISLANDS OF COHERENCE

Today, Wisdom Exchange has grown into a constellation of small, interconnected circles, each one sovereign yet connected by shared values, including the courage to remain engaged even when the conversation becomes difficult. Though most of our weekly circles meet virtually, they retain their sense of closeness and embodiment. What began informally has settled into a reliable rhythm for those involved. It has become a communal space where we speak from the heart, listen without trying to fix, and allow truth to arise from the relational field between us and, at times, from something that feels beyond any one of us.

Together, we've sat with grief, hope, the fear of collapse, and the longing for renewal. One evening, when a participant shared that he was considering leaving the country due to escalating political tensions, some expressed concern, others agreed, and still others saw things differently. However, no one argued, and no debate ensued. Instead, we shared the backgrounds that gave rise to our concerns. Through this commitment to relational intimacy, each voice offered a meaningful perspective, enriching the space between us. When the conversation ended, what remained wasn't certainty but relatedness. We experienced a felt sense of connection to one another and the larger complexity of the world. While no one walked away with answers, we all commented that we were leaving better than we had arrived, feeling more connected and more alive. Later, we shared that this embodied awareness stayed with us as we returned to our daily lives, beginning to shape how we lived.

This is what becomes possible when presence replaces performance. When we stop trying to persuade and instead allow ourselves to be fully present with ourselves and one another, we begin to sense into a deeper awareness—more profound and more fulfilling. We start to experience the meaning that lives between the words, in the subtle field of feeling and nuance where true transformation unfolds.

Within this relational field of awareness, change doesn't come from being convinced. It comes from being met. While meeting and being met in this loving way may not offer a quick fix for the complex crises we face, it is nonetheless a coherent shift. It is a reorientation within us that offers a way forward and, most importantly, a way forward together.

WHAT MAKES A WISDOM CIRCLE WORK

As my story about Wisdom Exchange illustrates, we don't need to have the right answers, a perfect life, or years of training to participate meaningfully in wisdom circles. What shapes our experience, and the experience of others, is how we show up—our willingness to be curious, to listen carefully, and to bring our embodied self into the communal space. These circles aren't about impressing one another with knowledge. They're about cultivating balanced attention, a capacity that feels rare in our fast-paced, performance-driven modern world.

When presence is grounded in a few essential relational qualities, like trust, sincerity, and humility, a remarkable shift begins to occur. The circle becomes more than a conversation. It transforms into a living field of shared intelligence. We can sense it in the atmosphere. It is quietly powerful and unmistakably communal, because we're participating in something larger than ourselves. When someone speaks from the heart, we notice ourselves leaning in, not to judge, but to truly feel what's being shared. In turn, we listen not just for content but for contact—for what is moving through the person and the relational space itself. This is how collective intelligence emerges, and there are several simple principles that can help a circle thrive in this way.[5]

Psychological Safety: Cultivating collective wisdom requires trust. But trust doesn't happen all at once. It grows over time through small, consistent signals, including committing to confidentiality, embodying kindness, and repairing ruptures. When we feel safe, we're more likely to disclose what is really going on for us. When honesty is met with care rather than judgment, transformation is possible.

Embodied Experience: In wisdom circles, we don't just speak from our heads; we also speak from our bodies, our hearts, and the lived experiences that carry meaning. There's a different texture to our words when we speak from experience rather than theory. It is more relatable and, therefore, lands more authentically. When our sharing resonates, we invite others to do the same.

Inquiry over Debate: These circles aren't arenas for winning arguments; they're sanctuaries for wondering out loud. Instead of rushing to conclusions or competing for the "right" answer, we practice curiosity. We ask questions and let them breathe. We explore together, trusting that clarity doesn't have to come quickly and that, frequently, the best answers are not answers at all but fuller ways of seeing and experiencing.

Attunement to Emergence: Usually, there is no fixed agenda or an expert at the front of the room to direct what happens. Instead, the group pays attention to what is arising within ourselves, between one another, and in the shared field among us. Slowly but reliably, insights deeper than any single perspective begin to take shape, especially when we're truly present together.

These principles aren't merely good communication tips. They are practices to be embodied and lived through. Like any true practice, they transform us over time as we engage them. Wisdom circles then become more than places of psychological or spiritual refuge, or sources of intellectual stimulation. They become communal spaces for birthing a different way of being for a different kind of world, one grounded in coherence and relational depth. Transformation occurs not necessarily through expertise, but through presence, care, and the simple yet radical act of listening well.

A HISTORICAL ECHO

We need not look far for evidence that this kind of relational container can change culture. In the mid-twentieth century, the Highlander Folk School in Tennessee embodied these very principles. A school known for its pivotal role in the civil rights movement, it was not a place of top-down instruction or rigid ideology. Instead, it functioned as a hearth for collective courage, a communal space where workers, teachers, and future civil rights leaders gathered to share stories, build trust, and imagine justice together.

What made Highlander so powerful was the cultivation of presence. Participants gathered in song, silence, and story, and wisdom emerged through it. They not only received an education but also took part in a reawakening of moral clarity grounded in relationship. Rosa Parks, for example, reconnected with her inner compass. As a result, she left with a stronger sense of coherence with something greater than herself and with the kind of inner alignment that would reverberate out and form a movement.[6]

Rather than changing history by force, Highlander nurtured people who could shape history themselves. This transformation emerged from the generative power of relational intelligence. In this way, Highlander became a living node of the Communal Heart, a fractal of coherence and courage pulsing through a fractured time.

FROM CIRCLES TO SYSTEMS

History reminds us that true transformation rarely arises from slogans, systems, or sweeping reforms. More often, it emerges through people learning to relate differently within small, coherent groups that weave their influence outward. Like the connective tissue of a living body, wisdom circles link individuals through invisible threads of trust, resonance, and shared insight, generating collective intelligence that leads to meaningful action.

Because these circles are made up of everyday people practicing generative ways of relating that are still rare in our culture, a single node of coherence can become contagious. As each circle attunes to its own rhythm and truth, it naturally begins to resonate with others. Over time, a living network forms, not through top-down authority but through relational alignment around a shared purpose. This is the hope at the center of the Communal Heart: Wherever people gather with sincerity and a willingness to trust, an intelligent field of connection begins to cohere our lives.

When this coherence ripples outward into our systems, our organizations, and our governance, a new kind of leadership begins to emerge, one that diverges from the familiar command-and-control style.[7] In its place, a more relational and attuned leadership is taking shape.[8] As we explored earlier in the book, this relational leadership is grounded, embodied, and wise. It listens before speaking, senses before acting, and leads by inviting others into their own agency. Rather than dominating or directing, it cultivates the conditions in which power is shared, and meaning can emerge.

And it begins right here—in small circles where courageous people are willing to meet one another with honesty and vulnerability and are changed by truly encountering one another. These spaces of belonging quietly prototype a kind of distributed leadership our times of crises demand.

In Chapter 14, we'll explore how small groups serve both as relational containers for healing and renewal and as the root system of a new cultural ecology. Linked by shared values, mutual care, and consistent responsiveness, they form a decentralized yet coherent field, a living network capable of sensing, evolving, and acting together. From these roots, a new form of governance is beginning to grow from the inside out.

Chapter 14
FROM ONE LIGHT COME MANY RAYS OF HOPE

The next Buddha may take the form of a community—
a community practicing understanding and loving-
kindness, a community practicing mindful living.
—Thich Nhat Hanh

We are living through a time of profound uncertainty. The systems that once offered predictability are faltering. The future can no longer be extrapolated from the past, because the conditions themselves are changing too quickly. In this nonlinear landscape, no single path forward is obvious. And yet, paradoxically, it is precisely this uncertainty that allows a deeper intelligence to surface. This intelligence doesn't rush to resolve but listens for resonance. In complex systems, coherence often precedes clarity.

The image of a prism helps illuminate this phenomenon. When light passes through a prism, the full spectrum of color becomes visible, not because anything new has been added, but because what was always present becomes perceptible through a transparent medium. In much the same way, the relational field of the Communal Heart, especially when trust is cultivated, reveals layered truths and diverse voices that often remain hidden beneath urgency and ideology. We begin to see not just more, but more fully. Not only what is, but also what is possible.

BRIGHT POSSIBILITIES OF BELONGING

We don't yet know which wavelengths will be most needed for a thriving future. We don't know which stories will heal, which technologies will endure, or which movements will grow into a lasting culture. But we can attune to the frequencies that resonate with life, those that carry care, coherence, courage, and curiosity.

Each small group that gathers with sincerity becomes a source of resonance, contributing its part to a distributed, relational intelligence. These gatherings may not resemble institutions or traditional leadership bodies. They may resist conventional measurement. Yet they are profoundly significant.

I recently heard about a group of community organizers responding to a local disaster. Over several evenings in a borrowed church hall, they sat in a circle, sharing grief, frustration, and flickers of hope. Without realizing it, they had become a prism of collective intelligence. One person's clarity about food distribution sparked another's idea for community refrigeration. A trauma therapist stepped forward to organize peer support, while a nurse offered medical attention for the wounded. No one directed the group, but slowly, coherence emerged. What formed wasn't a rigid plan but a living pattern, relational threads strong enough to meet the unknown together.

These kinds of circles don't begin with the answers. They begin with presence. Some will form around sorrow and repair, others around creativity and regeneration, and others still, around experimentation and innovation. They won't all sound and look the same. They don't need to. Their difference, held in coherence, is what gives them their strength and resiliency.

A FIELD OF MANY FUTURES

Wisdom circles are not an escape from the world. They are a return to a different way of being in it, a way that prepares us not only for inner transformation, but also for meaningful participation in a rapidly changing culture. The work we do in these relational spaces is not for us alone. It is a training ground for the very capacities our world is hungry for—for listening, discernment, holding tension, speaking truth without intentional harm, and acting from attuned clarity rather than reactive certainty. As these practices evolve, they begin to move outward, influencing how we parent, teach, build, repair, and govern. Small circles begin to shape cities. Communities learn to practice regenerative decision-making. And systems are guided less by external control and more by the coherence cultivated among people. This is how the Communal Heart becomes a cultural force, not by decree but by the light of embodied awareness moving through many lenses of perception, made visible wherever sincerity is present, and trust is possible.

In other words, what makes this time so pivotal is not that we know what to do, but that we are still capable of listening together for what is real. In the absence of certainty, coherence becomes the ground of possibility. While it may not offer a quick fix, relational intelligence can offer a more fulfilling way of sensing into what matters. And from this sensing, we begin to move away from rigid plans and with attuned presence toward responsiveness.

Therefore, the task before us isn't to construct a single future, but to cohere in such a way that many futures become possible. Futures rooted in trust. Futures carried by communities with the capacity to respond. Futures refracted through the courage to stay in relationship, even when it is uncomfortable. When we become living prisms, transparent enough for the light of consciousness to pass through and grounded enough to stay present amid complexity, we begin to reveal the full spectrum of what longs to be born.

Rather than a master plan consisting of traditional solutions, a mosaic composed of stories, circles, experiments, and embodied relationships is emerging. They are signals, evidence that presence, mutuality, and coherence are already shaping the culture to come. In Chapter 15, we'll explore where these resonant practices are already coming to life and how they are beginning to reshape how we relate, decide, organize, and lead.

Chapter 15
AN EMERGENT MOVEMENT GATHERING LIFE

Alone, we can go fast. Together, we can go far.
—African proverb

The journey we have taken through these pages has not unfolded as a straight line toward a fixed destination. Instead, it has unfolded as a spiral, drawing us back to ourselves, to one another, and to the living field of connection that holds us all. At the heart of this return lies what I've called the Communal Heart, a space of shared becoming that invites us to remember what it means to truly belong.

Along the way, we have begun to cultivate balanced attention, learning to respond to what this historical moment is asking of us. In doing so, we have seen how the fractures in our lives, systems, and culture can lead not only to disconnection and crisis but also to growth, especially in the generative tension where differences meet. In this meeting, we have come to appreciate that the integration of the mature masculine and the mature feminine, within ourselves and between us, opens a path forward that honors both discernment and compassion, and protection and nurturance.

From this deeper capacity for presence, we have explored how new relational spaces grounded in trust are beginning to take shape, serving as living containers for dialogue and relational coherence. Within these wisdom circles, we have discovered that a new kind of leadership can emerge, one that is more distributed and embodied, arising from the quality of attention and relationships people cultivate together.

Across the world, small but significant experiments in this kind of relational leadership are quietly taking place. They may not capture headlines, yet they are gradually reshaping the fabric of our shared life. In an era marked by complexity and fragmentation, these efforts offer more than inspiration. They demonstrate that cultural transformation is not only possible. It is already underway.

STEWARDING THE FIELD

In Antioquia, Colombia, amid the deep scars left by decades of armed conflict between guerrilla groups, paramilitaries, and the government, a group of farmers created what became known as the Peace Community of San José de Apartadó.[1] For years, they endured violence, displacement, and the constant threat of retribution from all sides. However, in 1997, amid this turmoil, they made a radical choice. Instead of fleeing or taking up arms in retaliation, they chose a different path. They turned toward one another for support, courage, and guidance, trusting that peace could be cultivated not through force, but through the strength of their shared humanity.

This community offers a living example of relational leadership in action. As political tensions rose and their community felt increasing pressure to respond, their approach to decision-making was grounded in mutual trust and a profound commitment to nonviolence. Through collective gatherings such as wisdom circles, they developed collective decision-making processes and cultivated the land together as acts of both survival and resistance. Leadership rotated among members, and decisions were made in open assemblies. There was no single charismatic figure imposing a vision, only a common understanding that coherence was the foundation of their strength.

Rather than seek revenge for the atrocities they had endured, they chose to live in a way that modeled peace. Remarkably, their relational stance extended not only to one another but also to the land that sustained them, to honoring their ancestors who came before, and to the future generations whose well-being they actively protected. Their coherence became their resilience. Their refusal to perpetuate cycles of violence became a moral compass. And their fortitude became a practical anchor for others in the region and beyond.

The Peace Community did more than survive; they revealed what becomes possible when leadership is grounded in relationship, when decisions arise through dialogue, and when love is not merely a sentiment but a shared and sustained practice. Even in the most fragmented landscapes and political systems, they demonstrated that relational integrity can be a force more powerful than fear.[2]

This is the emergent movement of relational intelligence. It does not always make the news, but it almost always changes lives, and, over time, it changes systems from the inside out. And it is already underway, developing in ordinary places among ordinary people, who become extraordinary through this work of relational wisdom.

CULTIVATING BELONGING AS SHARED GOVERNANCE

In Taiwan, digital minister Audrey Tang is modeling this new kind of relational leadership on the international stage. Known for radical transparency and collaborative governance, Tang facilitates open-source democracy platforms that invite public participation and shared authorship of public policy. Citizens not only comment on proposed laws; they also help create them. In this model of distributive democracy, leadership is less a top-down performance of power and much more a responsive, facilitative process that listens carefully and adapts dynamically. Tang's work is therefore shaped by coherence and collaborative work grounded in the ability to integrate diverse inputs into meaningful collective action. It is a living demonstration of what becomes possible when leadership is rooted in the wisdom of the communal whole rather than the control of a few.[3]

Even in places like Bowling Green, Kentucky, this shift toward relational leadership is steadily taking hold. In a community that has historically grappled with rapid growth, industrial expansion, and evolving demographics, its own town halls have been reimagined as spaces of relational deliberation, where residents are encouraged to come together not just to be heard but also to hear one another. These gatherings move beyond venting or debate. They become containers for collective insight, where differences are met with curiosity rather than defensiveness.

Policy about affordable housing, for instance, is no longer imposed from above. It is being co-created. More recently, the What Could BG Be? initiative allowed residents of Warren County, Kentucky, to use an online platform powered by artificial intelligence to contribute over a million responses and shape the community's twenty-five-year strategic vision, transforming traditional policy formation into a large-scale co-creative process. In this way, trust, so often eroded in civic life, is slowly being restored.[4]

A VILLAGE OF COHERENCE

Meanwhile, on the other side of the United States, a different expression of relational governance is taking shape in San Francisco. At Frontier Tower, a sixteen-story building has been transformed by German entrepreneurs Jakob Drzazga, Christian Nagel, and Christian Peters, into what its participants call a *vertical village*. Originally a hub for frontier technologies, the space now functions as a living network of coherence, bringing together AI researchers, biotech innovators, artists, regenerative designers, and community builders into sustained proximity. Each floor hosts its own theme, but all are held together through intentional culture-building and mutual respect.[5]

Rather than centralized leadership or top-down direction, decision-making unfolds through open dialogue, shared meals, participatory design, and collective sensemaking. It is an eco-system of self-organizing, collaborative practice that mirrors the dynamics of wisdom circles but is scaled vertically across disciplines and domains.

However, the Frontier Tower isn't a polished prototype, and that is precisely the point. It embraces emergence as its guiding principle. It is a microcosm of what becomes possible when relational coherence is taken seriously as a civic and cultural foundation. In a city often marked by fragmentation, it offers a model of what it means to govern from the inside out, to let resonance shape response, and to allow difference to become a source of strength rather than division.

THE WORLD WE MAKE POSSIBLE

From the mountainous villages of Colombia to the digital platforms of Taiwan, from small-town Kentucky to a vertical village in San Francisco, rays of hope are becoming visible. In addition to being a personal capacity, relational coherence is also a cultural force. It emerges wherever people practice presence, listen deeply, and lead with care. It does not arise from dominance or control, but from the subtle, consistent work of tending the relational space between us. Whether through wisdom circles, civic assemblies, or experimental communities, an essential truth radiates through them all: How we attend, perceive, and relate determines what becomes possible and, ultimately, the world we leave to future generations.

An Invitation to Practice the Communal Heart in Action

Let us hold this return to the Communal Heart as a beginning, a sacred threshold calling us to live from the deep belonging that has always been our true inheritance. The Communal Heart is our birthright and a path to be lived into. Ideas alone do not change the world; they are transformed by *how* we embody them.

Check-In: Are You Resonating with Others?

With a trusted friend, colleague, neighbor, or family member, inquire into the following:

- When was a time we showed up for ourselves and one another?
- How do we navigate uncertainty without collapsing into fear or the illusion of control?
- How do we build trust and coherence in an increasingly fragmented world?

I invite you to use these questions, along with the guidelines at the end of the book, as a simple way to begin a wisdom circle of your own.

Epilogue
IT STARTS WITH US

We are the ones we have been waiting for.
—Alice Walker

As we enter the wide adoption of artificial intelligence and increasingly sophisticated systems of simulated thought, we are being invited to reflect more deeply on what it means to be human. AI, and the large language models through which it operates, can mimic certain forms of intelligence. It can process vast amounts of information, recognize patterns, and generate coherent responses in seconds. But it cannot create meaning through the tender, embodied experience of being alive. It cannot feel, take risks, or enter into relationship as we do. It cannot, therefore, offer the kind of genuine connection we so urgently need to meet the personal and collective challenges of our time.

What we now need is to temper technological acceleration with an appreciation for mutuality—the relational intelligence that arises through the willingness to be changed by one another.

We must not forget this.

While tech firms have long mined our attention, treating it as a commodity to be captured and sold, they are turning their sights toward an even more precious commodity: our longing for intimacy. Already, we are being offered artificial companions—personal assistants that make life easier but never call us into greater maturity, psychotherapists that reflect our words but do not help us integrate the meaning behind them, coaches that cheer us on but never risk telling us the truth, and romantic partners that offer validation but not the embodied mutuality that helps us grow. These systems are designed to keep us engaged by saying exactly what we want to hear, but not always what we need to hear. Because AI is fundamentally designed to operate in one direction—from it to us.

True intimacy does not grow solely through agreement or affirmation. What deepens us and matures the relational field is the shared willingness to be transformed by the presence of another. What I hope this book has revealed is that real intimacy asks something of us. It challenges our assumptions. It stretches our capacity to stay, listen, and love, even in the face of uncertainty.

Simulated intimacy cannot offer this. Though it may promise seamless connection—free from rupture, awkwardness, or risk—that ease comes at a cost. Without friction, there can be no real growth. Without nuance or vulnerability, there can be no transformation or mutual becoming. The danger is not merely that AI might replace human relationships, but that it will offer simulations so convincing we choose them instead. And if we do, we may lose our appetite for the very messy, unpredictable, and beautifully real aliveness that genuine intimacy requires.

If current trends continue and tech companies succeed in bringing AI companions into every home and every heart, it is not difficult to imagine a future where engaging with a machine is more convenient, perhaps even more desirable, than relating to another human being. What we have, then, is a future where efficiency replaces empathy and predictability outpaces presence. It does not take much to imagine where that road leads, toward a slow erosion of relational capacity and a diminishing of what it means to be truly seen, known, and changed by another.

The task before us is monumental, not because the machines are powerful, but because the human heart is precious. To meet this moment with integrity, we must reclaim the value of human presence. We must choose the living, breathing texture of real connection over the smooth veneer of artificial intimacy. The future of our relationships, and perhaps of our humanity, could very well depend on our doing so.

Lived, relational wisdom will guide us through the great unknowns ahead, calling us back to our belonging with one another and with the natural world. This is why relational intelligence is not a luxury; it is a necessity. It forms the foundation of collective resilience, emotional depth, and moral clarity, capacities no machine can replicate.

And so, we return again to what is essential—to the sanctity of relationship, the beauty of being with one another, and the steady power of showing up, heart open, to the miracle of being alive in a world of belonging.

THIS IS OUR JOURNEY

As you move forward, remember that the Communal Heart does not need to be invented or built from scratch. It is already here, alive and pulsing in the space between us, waiting to be revealed and lived into. You do not have to go far to find it. You have only to return to it.

Even when the path feels uncertain, you are not alone. You are connected to others, to the Earth, and to the wisdom that moves through relationship itself. Every act of presence carries weight. Every moment of genuine care extends outward in ways you may never fully see. Yet each time you return to the field of belonging with openness and humility, you strengthen the invisible weave that holds us all together.

The world we long for is not a fantasy. It is a living possibility, one that depends not on perfect systems or heroic individuals but on our collective willingness to relate, to cohere, and to lead from love. Step gently but boldly. Stay close to what is real. Keep returning. Keep listening. Keep loving. Let the Communal Heart become more than a metaphor. Let it become your way of being.

A FINAL INVITATION TO PRACTICE

I leave you with a final practice: These questions are not only reflections for the mind. They are invitations for the heart and guidance for the soul. They are doorways into the many layers of relational life and gateways into the collective wisdom we are longing to remember and restore. Most importantly, they are seeds of the next culture, already taking root beneath the surface of modern life.

- What do you truly value, not just in theory but also in practice, in the choices you make each day?

- Whom do you trust enough to explore those values with you, to hold you accountable to what matters most?
- How do you recognize value for its own sake—in others, in yourself, in the more-than-human world around you?

The world transforms when insight is embodied, when care becomes action, and when presence becomes more than a practice but a way of life.

WISDOM CIRCLE GUIDELINES

A wisdom circle is a space of relational coherence. It is a living field where presence, trust, and inquiry invite collective intelligence to emerge.

FORMING A CIRCLE

- **Connect:** Gather three to seven people online or in person, or both.
- **Commit:** Meet regularly (weekly, biweekly, monthly).
- **Create:** Choose a quiet space free of distraction, ideally in a circle, where each voice is equal.

SHARED AGREEMENTS

- **Real Identities:** Especially when meeting online, agree to keep cameras on and use full names and current locations to help the group ground its interactions in the felt sense of relatedness from which social trust can form.

- **Presence:** Arrive as you are and let distractions fall away.
- **Confidentiality:** Commit to keeping what is shared in the circle in the circle, unless permitted to do otherwise.
- **Non-Fixing:** Witness, rather than advise, unless asked to.
- **Mutual Inquiry:** Ask questions together, not to find the right answer but to deepen mutual awareness and understanding.
- **Repair:** Commit to tending to rupture with care and humility, seeking support from other group members if necessary.
- **Emergence:** Honor the emergent field between group members, listening for when someone is called to speak and remaining silent when silence beckons, recognizing that collective intelligence that emerges within the group is often wiser than any one person could have come up with on their own.

GROUP PROCESS

1. **Choose a Facilitator:** This person stewards the circle's relational flow, making sure everyone is included while midwifing the wisdom being born among everyone.
2. **Hide Self-View:** If meeting online, consider hiding your self-view to reduce distraction and to better simulate the experience of being together in real life.

3. **Turn Audio On:** Keep your microphone on to help sustain a verbal connection.
4. **Centering Practice:** Cultivate presence through awareness practices.
5. **Opening Check-In:** Briefly share how you're arriving.
6. **Shared Inquiry:** Pose a central question or allow a theme to emerge.
7. **Harvest:** Finish by exploring what stood out. What was touched? What needs finishing or repairing?
8. **Closing:** Close with gratitude, intention, or silence.

GLOSSARY OF CORE TERMS

Archetypal Energy: General patterns of perception and participation found across cultures and stories over time. While feminine and masculine energies have biological roots, they also live within each of us.

Attention: Essentially, it is how we look. It moves through awareness and functions like an aperture—widening or narrowing, focusing or relaxing—selecting what comes into the foreground.

Attractor: A gravitational center of meaning or behavior that pulls individuals, groups, or societies in a particular direction over time.

Attunement: The capacity for deeply listening to and resonating with others, the environment, and one's own inner experience.

Awareness: The spacious, receptive field that allows us to sense what is emerging within and among us. It reflects the holding capacity often associated with the feminine. From awareness come choice, trust, and responsiveness.

Belonging: A felt sense of connection and acceptance within oneself and with the greater web of life, including the natural world.

Coherence: The ability to regulate ourselves while co-regulating with others so that our collective actions align with what each situation calls for to support sustainability. Along with presence and mutuality, coherence forms one of the three relational capacities cultivated on the path into the Communal Heart.

Collective Intelligence: The emergent wisdom that arises when people come together with shared intention, care, and trust.

Communal Heart, the: The relational field of shared intelligence, rooted in presence and the process of love, that lives within, between, among us, and even beyond.

Contact Cycle: A model from Gestalt therapy describing the natural phases of engagement from rest to emergence, mobilization, contact, assimilation, satisfaction, withdrawal, and integration. This cycle of change supports wholeness in human experience and the natural world.

Creative Communion: The state of being that arises when people co-regulate and, in turn, co-create from a place of mutual presence, trust, and alignment. It transcends transaction and awakens shared imagination and purpose.

Developmental Lens: A framework for understanding how individuals and cultures evolve in complexity, relational capacity, and consciousness over time. Includes traditional, modern, postmodern, and metamodern/integrative stages; each offering distinct strengths and limitations, none is inherently better than the other.

Embodied Practice: Any practice that integrates bodily awareness with attention, emotion, and relational presence. Includes breathwork, somatic tracking, bodily movement, and grounded listening.

Field (Relational Field): The invisible but felt web of connection within, between, and among individuals and the non-human world. Includes emotional tone, body language, interpersonal communication, and energetic presence that shape the shared space.

Fractal Coherence: A recursive pattern by which small, coherent systems (like wisdom circles) reflect and influence larger systems, showing that relational integrity at the micro level can ripple out to systemic change.

Generative Dialogue: A form of conversation where participants listen deeply and co-create meaning together, allowing something new to emerge between them that is greater than the sum of their perspectives and insights combined.

Gestalt Practice: An awareness practice developed by Dick Price at the Esalen Institute to become more fully aware of the process of living within a unified field of body, mind, and spirit.

Holding the Field: The practice of sustaining a coherent, safe, and attuned relational space in which others can unfold, speak truth, or heal. Often used by facilitators and leaders of wisdom circles.

Immediacy: The capacity to sense and respond to what is arising in the moment, both within and between us.

Inner Work: The personal journey of healing, self-awareness, and integration necessary for relational maturity.

Integration: The process of bringing disparate parts of the self or system together into a meaningful, functional whole.

Love: While it can be romantic and sentimental, at its deepest, love is the process of knowing and being known, from which something entirely new emerges, transcending and including the parts while becoming greater than their sum.

Mature Masculine/Feminine: Natural energies found in all of us—structure and flow, doing and being, discernment and care—each essential and incomplete without the other.

Metacrisis: Beneath all the world's major crises lies a shared confusion born from the material and spiritual burnout of modern life. This underlying delusion manifests in our ways of thinking and behavior, shaping many of the interconnected problems that now threaten life on Earth.

Mutuality: A reciprocal connection and phenomenon of affecting and being affected. The realization that we are all interconnected. Along with presence and coherence, mutuality forms one of the three relational capacities cultivated on the path into the Communal Heart.

Perception: The kind of world that shows up as a result of how we are attending. Essentially, it is what we see.

Presence: The quality of being fully here: embodied, aware, and open to what is. It is embodied awareness with attention held in balance. The foundation of relational intelligence, presence is a recognition of mutuality and the basis of coherence. Along with mutuality and coherence, presence forms one of the three relational capacities cultivated on the path into the Communal Heart.

Quantity/Quality: While quantity means a fixed number of something and is therefore of *extrinsic value* (valued as a means to an end, like money), quality is of *intrinsic value* (valued for its own sake, such as a loved one).

Reality: Not only a fixed or objective state "out there," but also a living, dynamic process that unfolds through relationships within, between, and among us and even beyond.

Reconciling Force: That which transforms polarity into possibility. Not compromise but emergence.

Relatedness: The felt sense that we are always in relationship with ourselves, one another, the Earth, and the larger systems that we shape and that shape us, all the time, all at once.

Relational (to be): A way of being that honors the body, heart, and mind as equally valid centers of knowing, rooted in present-moment connection.

Relational Field: The space of shared perception, emotion, and meaning between people and the non-human world. This field can be fractured or coherent, depending on the quality of attention, trust, and care present.

Relational Intelligence: The capacity to listen, feel, sense, and respond wisely within relationships.

Relational Intimacy: The process of sharing the ground (or background of meaning) from which our behaviors arise, which gives "what" its meaning.

Relational Maturity: The capacity to stay grounded, listen deeply, navigate difference, and respond wisely in relationships, especially under stress or rupture. It reflects inner development expressed outwardly. It is integration made visible.

Relational Wisdom: The lived intelligence that emerges through experiences of attunement, response, and integration to self, others, and the living world. In essence, wisdom is the capacity to perceive reality clearly and respond to it with integrity.

Relationality: The fact that we are always in relationship, and so is everything else.

Resilience: The capacity to metabolize rupture into wisdom.

Resonance: The shared vibration of aliveness that emerges through integration as we attune and cohere within ourselves and between us.

Responsiveness: The capacity to be with what is and to respond to what the situation requires with care for self, other, and the non-human world.

Rupture and Repair: The cycle through which trust is restored after disconnection. There is a recognition that conflict is inevitable, yet coherence can be formed through courageous return and attuned repair.

Small Islands of Coherence: Small, interconnected groups of trusted companions who engage in generative dialogue to make sense of the world together, cultivating collective wisdom in the process.

Threshold: A liminal space or moment of transition that holds potential for transformation and emergence.

Wisdom Circle: A small group of no more than seven people committed to relational practice, mutual inquiry, and collective presence.

ACKNOWLEDGMENTS

I want to extend my heartfelt gratitude to those whose support was vital in bringing this book to life:

First, to the many clients I have worked with over three decades of psychotherapy: Thank you for trusting me with your stories. This book was largely born from what I learned about the nuances of the human heart while sitting with you.

To my esteemed publishing team at Wonderwell Press, particularly Maggie Langrick, Brian Welch, Tess Newton, Sheila McMullin, Jeffery Curry, Divine Byrd, Sheila Parr, Brittany Jones-Pugh, Rachel High, Brady Powers, and Kyle Pearson: Your technical expertise and insightful reflections kept me committed to this project, even when it felt out of reach.

To my writing coaches, Wendy Jane Carrel, Carolyn Bond, and Martha Woolverton: Your honest and generous support allowed me to move beyond the first draft.

To my colleagues and friends, Jim Palmer, Joe Lightfoot, Steven Harper, Simon Divecha, Jeff Williams, Manuel Manga, Robert Kelley Ayala, God'swill Osa, Jochen Weber, Daniel VanderBijl, Jasen Robillard, Kevin Triplett, Marty Behrens, and John Stokdijk: Your thoughtful reflections and consistent encouragement helped this work find its way into a wider community.

To the entire Wisdom Exchange community, you have become like family to me: Thank you for trusting me to facilitate difficult yet compassionate conversations and for believing that our little communal experiment in the art of belonging makes a difference in the world.

To my mentor, Lucie Chalifour: I am deeply grateful for the grace with which you midwife my relationship with the Ineffable. Thank you for your steadfast friendship and enduring maternal love.

To my dear sons, Noah and Luke, through whom I have learned what it means to truly be human: You keep me curious, open, and honest amid both your changes and mine. I feel so fortunate to be your mother.

And last but certainly not least, to my husband, Peter, without whom I would be only half the woman I am today. To you, my constant companion, reliable muse, best friend, and forever love: I give you my heart and cherish your soul.

NOTES

Preface

Epigraph: Clarissa Pinkola Estés, "Do Not Lose Heart, We Were Made for These Times," *Moon Magazine*, 2016, http://moonmagazine.org/clarissa-pinkola-estes-do-not-lose-heart-we-were-made-for-these-times-2016-12-31/.

Introduction: The Heart We Have Forgotten

Epigraph: Though not a direct quote, this is widely attributed to Pierre Teilhard de Chardin, based on an interpretation of his broader themes on evolution, hope, and the future of humanity, found in Pierre Teilhard de Chardin, *The Phenomenon of Man* (Harper, 1955).

1. From John Koetsier, "80% Of Gen Zers Would Marry an AI: Study," *Forbes*, April 29, 2025, https://www.forbes.com/sites/johnkoetsier/2025/04/29/80-of-gen-zers-would-marry-an-ai-study/.
2. See, for example: IPCC, *AR6 Synthesis Report: Climate Change 2023* (Intergovernmental Panel on Climate Change), documenting accelerating climate disruption; World Inequality Lab, *World Inequality Report 2022*, detailing widening global and national economic inequality; U.S. Surgeon General Vivek H. Murthy, *Our Epidemic of Loneliness and Isolation* (2023), identifying loneliness as a major public health concern; and Pew Research Center, *Political Polarization in the American Public* (latest editions), documenting rising social and ideological polarization.
3. The term "metacrisis" was first introduced by the French philosopher Edgar Morin to describe a crisis beneath and between multiple crises, specifically a breakdown at levels of meaning, knowledge, and coordination. Edgar Morin, *Pour une crisologie* (du Seuil, 1976).
4. Wisdom Exchange (WE) is an international community that I founded in 2023. It consists of small, interconnected, trust-based groups dedicated

to cultivating relational presence, generative dialogue, and shared inquiry. Through regular gatherings and reflective practices, participants explore how embodied awareness and relatedness can support personal integration and collective coherence during cultural transition.

5. The field of belonging can be understood as a field of relationality—what Buber (1958) calls the "between," what Siegel (2012) describes as the relational nature of mind, and what Gestalt field theory (Perls, Hefferline, and Goodman, 1951) frames as the co-emergent space in which experience arises. Martin Buber, *I and Thou*, 2nd ed. (Charles Scribner's Sons, 1958); D. J. Siegel, *The Developing Mind: How Relationships and the Brain Interact to Shape Who We Are*, 2nd ed. (Guilford Press, 2012); Frederick S. Perls, Ralph Hefferline, and Paul Goodman, *Gestalt Therapy: Excitement and Growth in the Human Personality* (Julian Press, 1951).
6. Sex essentially refers to our biological makeup. At the genetic level, this means chromosomes: typically, XX (female) or XY (male). While chromosomal variations exist (such as XXY or XO), the vast majority of people are born with one or the other.

   Sex also shows up at the phenotypic level—that is, our morphology, or outward expression of sex, including genitalia and secondary sexual characteristics. When a baby is "assigned" a sex at birth, that designation is based almost entirely on phenotype. Science has shown, however, that genotype and phenotype do not always match, which is why intersex conditions exist.

   Gender is more complex. It refers both to one's felt sense of being male, female, both, or neither, as well as to the social roles, expectations, and norms associated with those categories. Gender, in this sense, has both biological underpinnings (influenced by hormones and neurology) and social dimensions (shaped by culture, norms, and history). Both influence our psychology and our ways of relating to others.

   Increasingly, people are reporting that their gender identity diverges from the sex assigned to them at birth. Some of this may be due to cultural shifts that make it safer for people to speak openly. Some may be the influence of society itself. The truth is, we do not yet fully understand all the factors at play. What we do know is that transgender people exist, and their lived experience offers all of us valuable insights into what it might be like to inhabit the biological, psychological, and social realities of the other sex. Not only is this important for those individuals themselves; it also expands our collective capacity for empathy and understanding.

7. The term "archetypal energetic" refers to the universal patterns of psychological and relational experience that arise from the archetypes of the collective unconscious, the primordial forms that shape human behavior, perception, and meaning-making across cultures. These archetypal patterns often reveal themselves as energetic tendencies or directional impulses within the psyche, influencing how we attend, act, relate, and make sense of experience. Carl G. Jung, trans. R. F. C. Hull, *The Archetypes and the Collective Unconscious* (Princeton University Press, 1968).

Chapter 1: When Attention Splits

Epigraph: While this quote is widely attributed to Albert Einstein, its exact origin in his writings or speeches remains unverified.

1. David McIlroy, "Understanding Iain McGilchrist's Worldview," *Perspectiva*, Substack, January 25, 2024, https://perspecteeva.substack.com/p/understanding-iain-mcgilchrists-worldview. McIlory points out, "In unhealthy individuals, groups, and societies, the move to isolate and manipulate is the primary move, and the left hemisphere creates a feedback loop that fails to acknowledge the reality of that which can be embraced but cannot be grasped, that which must be accepted but cannot be captured in words. McGilchrist's argument is that healthy individuals, groups, and societies approach the world first via the right hemisphere, reacting to what is found there to form an impression of how everything links together; then the left hemisphere looks in detail at elements that can become objects of human action in isolation, and then the results of the left hemisphere's inspection are returned to the right hemisphere where the individual elements are reintegrated into a more profound understanding of the whole."
2. Iain McGilchrist, *The Master and His Emissary: The Divided Brain and the Making of the Western World* (Yale University Press, 2009). In *The Master and His Emissary*, McGilchrist explores how the two hemispheres of the brain attend to the world in fundamentally different ways. He argues that the right hemisphere (the "Master") perceives reality in a broad, contextual, and relational manner, while the left hemisphere (the "Emissary") tends to abstract, fragment, and control. McGilchrist traces how Western culture has increasingly privileged the left hemisphere's mode of attention, leading to a loss of connection, coherence, and, ultimately, meaning. His work offers a compelling framework for understanding the cultural fragmentation and reductionism that underlie many of today's crises, including those in healthcare, education, and ecology.

3. Rong Su, James Rounds, and Patrick Ian Armstrong, "Men and Things, Women and People: A Meta-Analysis of Sex Differences in Interests," *Psychological Bulletin* 135, no. 6 (November 2009): 859–884.

   Moreover, research suggests that in highly egalitarian societies, such as those in Scandinavia, individuals are more empowered to pursue careers that align with their interests and preferences. Under these conditions of greater freedom, many women tend to gravitate toward fields that are less technical and more people-oriented, like healthcare and education. This pattern supports the view that gendered differences in interests may be influenced less by socialization and more by underlying biological tendencies. Gijsbert Stoet and David C. Geary, "The Gender-Equality Paradox in Science, Technology, Engineering, and Mathematics Education," *Psychological Science* 29, no. 4 (February 2018): 581–593.

4. While these patterns reflect historical tendencies rather than fixed biological destinies—and while both modes of attention are present in all individuals and become most generative when held in relationship rather than assigned or opposed—these ideas draw upon well-established scientific findings in evolutionary psychology, developmental neuroscience, and attachment theory and have been discussed by a number of scholars:

   John Bowlby, *Attachment and Loss, vol. 1: Attachment*, 2nd ed. (Basic Books, 1982).

   Mary D. S. Ainsworth et al., *Patterns of Attachment: A Psychological Study of the Strange Situation* (Erlbaum, 1978).

   Ruth Feldman, "Parent–Infant Synchrony and the Construction of Shared Timing," *Journal of Child Psychology and Psychiatry* 48, nos. 3–4 (2007): 329–354.

   Sarah Blaffer Hrdy, *Mothers and Others: The Evolutionary Origins of Mutual Understanding* (Harvard University Press, 2009).

   David C. Geary, *Male, Female: The Evolution of Human Sex Differences*, 2nd ed. (American Psychological Association, 2010).

   Mark Van Vugt, David De Cremer, and Dirk P. Janssen, "Gender Differences in Cooperation and Competition: The Male-Warrior Hypothesis," *Psychological Science* 18, no. 1 (2007): 19–23.

5. In the United States, women gained the constitutional right to vote with the ratification of the Nineteenth Amendment in 1920; see Alexander Keyssar, *The Right to Vote: The Contested History of Democracy in the United States*, rev. ed. (Basic Books, 2009), 193–221. Comparative research shows that across modern Western societies, women's suffrage emerged late in the process of democratization—most often in the late nineteenth or twentieth centuries,

frequently following prolonged activism, social upheaval, or war—indicating that modern liberal democracies initially defined political agency in explicitly male terms; see Pamela Paxton, Melanie M. Hughes, and Tiffany M. Barnes, *Women, Politics, and Power: A Global Perspective*, 3rd ed. (Rowman & Littlefield, 2021), 27–54; Jad Adams, *Women and the Vote: A World History* (Oxford: Oxford University Press, 2014). For representative timelines, see New Zealand (1893), the United Kingdom (partial suffrage in 1918; equal suffrage in 1928), the United States (1920), France (1944), and Switzerland (1971). The delayed extension of voting rights to women reflects a broader pattern in which modern political institutions were structured around male-coded assumptions of rationality, agency, and public authority, while women's roles were largely confined to the private sphere; see Carole Pateman, *The Sexual Contract* (Stanford University Press, 1988), 1–18.

6. Iain McGilchrist does not explicitly frame hemispheric differences in terms of maternal attunement and paternal protectiveness. However, his account of evolutionarily shaped modes of attention, developed most fully in *The Master and His Emissary*, argues that the hemispheres differ not in what they do, but in how they attend. The application of this attentional distinction to early caregiving contexts represents an interpretive extension consistent with McGilchrist's framework rather than a claim he makes directly.
7. While Iain McGilchrist describes our modern tendency to favor the narrow, analytical attention of the left hemisphere, which sidelines the relational, holistic awareness of the right hemisphere, this imbalance can be understood as a form of "left-hemispheric chauvinism," a cultural bias that elevates abstraction, categorization, and control over presence, context, and connection.
8. Hanzi Freinacht, *The Listening Society: A Metamodern Guide to Politics: Book One* (Metamoderna, 2017).

Chapter 2: Where We Come Pulled Apart

Epigraph: John Muir, *My First Summer in the Sierra* (Houghton Mifflin, 1911).

1. World Health Organization, "'Depression: Let's Talk' Says WHO, as Depression Tops List of Causes of Ill Health," March 30, 2017, https://www.who.int/news/item/30-03-2017--depression-let-s-talk-says-who-as-depression-tops-list-of-causes-of-ill-health.

2. Rory Arnold, "Neighbors Want Deeper Connections. What's Holding Them Back?," *Rocket Mortgage*, February 19, 2026, https://www.rocketmortgage.com.
3. Gerardo Ceballos, Paul R. Ehrlich, et al., "Accelerated Modern Human–Induced Species Losses: Entering the Sixth Mass Extinction," *Science Advances* 1, no. 5 (June 2015): e1400253.
4. Intergovernmental Panel on Climate Change, *Climate Change 2023 Synthesis Report: Summary for Policymakers* (IPCC, 2023), https://www.ipcc.ch/report/ar6/syr/downloads/report/IPCC_AR6_SYR_SPM.pdf.
5. National Research Council, *The Growth of Incarceration in the United States: Exploring Causes and Consequences* (National Academies Press, 2014).
6. Jahneille Cunningham, "Missing the Mark: Standardized Testing as Epistemological Erasure in U.S. Schooling," *Power and Education* 11, no. 1 (March 2019): 111–120.
7. Flavie Halais, "Want to Fix Urban Sprawl? Ditch the Cul-de-Sac," *WIRED*, May 31, 2020, https://www.wired.com/story/fix-urban-sprawl-ditch-cul-de-sac/.

Chapter 3: How We Find Our Way Home

Epigraph: While this quote is commonly attributed to Kabir's oral poetic tradition of the 15th century, wording varies across sources.

Chapter 4: In Rhythm with Nature

Epigraph: An excerpt from an April 1985 interview with Dick Price, conducted by Wade Hudson at the Esalen Institute.

1. The Gestalt Legacy Project, *Manual of Gestalt Practice in the Tradition of Dick Price*, rev. ed. (Lulu.com, 2014).
2. Joseph Zinker, *Creative Process in Gestalt Therapy* (Brunner/Mazel, 1977).
3. I want to thank Steven Harper for helping me learn to integrate this basic awareness practice into both my professional and my personal life.

Chapter 5: The Practice of Being Here

Epigraph: Eckhart Tolle, *A New Earth: Awakening to Your Life's Purpose* (Dutton, 2005).

1. Research in personality psychology and communication studies suggests that, on average, women tend to score higher on agreeableness and empathic attunement, while men are more likely to adopt problem-solving approaches in relational contexts—patterns that reflect statistical tendencies rather than fixed traits. David P. Schmitt, Robert Jüri Allik, Robert R. McCrae, and Veronica Benet-Martínez, "The Geographic Distribution of Big Five Personality Traits: Patterns and Profiles of Human Self-Description Across 56 Nations," *Journal of Cross-Cultural Psychology* 38, no. 2 (2007): 173–212.
2. Awareness, Choice, and Trust are considered the "The Three Jewels" of Gestalt Practice, a term identified by Dick Price and later adapted by Steven Harper. In their model, choice is synonymous with choosing and therefore includes respond-ability or responsiveness.
3. In Iain McGilchrist, *The Master and His Emissary: The Divided Brain and the Making of the Western World* (Yale University Press, 2009), McGilchrist expresses this process of analysis and reality testing, which consists of the "right, left, right" hemispheric functioning, as "all that is to be known must initially be 'presenced' to the right hemisphere (we have no other access); then be transferred to the left hemisphere so as to gain expression through re-presentation; and that re-presentation returned to the right hemisphere where it is either recognised for its consonance with the initial presencing and subsumed into a new *Gestalt*, or rejected." Jonathan Rowson identifies this careful calibration as the "McGilchrist Manoeuvre." Jonathan Rowson, "Introducing the McGilchrist Manoeuvre," *The Joyous Struggle*, Substack, March 1, 2023, https://jonathanrowson.substack.com/p/introducing-the-mcgilchrist-manoeuvre.
4. Ludwig Wittgenstein, *Philosophical Investigations*, trans. G. E. M. Anscombe, P. M. S. Hacker, and Joachim Schulte, rev. 4th ed. (Malden, MA: Wiley-Blackwell, 2009), 194e–195e.

Chapter 6: Rewriting the Stories We Inherit

Epigraph: Don Richard Riso and Russ Hudson, *The Wisdom of the Enneagram: The Complete Guide to Psychological and Spiritual Growth for the Nine Personality Types* (Bantam, 1999).

1. The Enneagram offers a comprehensive map for identifying and then

transforming the strategies we learned early in our lives for securing worth, safety, and belonging.

2. Internal Family Systems, developed by Richard C. Schwartz, is a widely practiced form of psychotherapy where different aspects of the self, often called "parts," are identified, explored, and eventually integrated into a greater sense of wholeness. Richard C. Schwartz, *Internal Family Systems Therapy* (Guilford Press, 1995).
3. These messages are informed by the Enneagram, a map of how personality organizes our lives. Riso and Hudson, *The Wisdom of the Enneagram.*
4. My colleague, Steven Harper, a Gestalt Practitioner, works with messages received early in life. He helps those he works with identify the unconscious programs and filters that shape their perception and supports them in updating these messages to better reflect their current circumstances.

Chapter 7: Those Who Help Us Become

Epigraph: John O'Donohue, *Anam Ćara: A Book of Celtic Wisdom* (Harper Perennial, 1997).

1. A soul friendship is rooted in mutual recognition, trust, and presence, where the soul is free to be truly seen. O'Donohue, *Anam Ćara.*

Chapter 8: The Art of Generative Exchange

Epigraph: Theodore Zeldin, *Conversation: How Talk Can Change Our Lives* (HiddenSpring, 1998).

1. Martin Buber, *I and Thou*, trans. Walter Kaufmann (Charles Scribner's Sons, 1970).
2. The Gestalt Legacy Project, *Manual of Gestalt Practice in the Tradition of Dick Price*, rev. ed. (Lulu.com, 2014).
3. Jeremy D. Safran, J. Christopher Muran, and Catherine Eubanks-Carter, "Repairing Alliance Ruptures," *Psychotherapy* 48, no. 1 (March 2011): 80–87.
4. Timotheus Vermeulen and Robin van den Akker, "Notes on Metamodernism," *Journal of Aesthetics & Culture* 2, no. 1 (2010): 1–14.

Chapter 9: Cracks That Bring Us Closer

1. Céline Santini, *Kintsugi: Finding Strength in Imperfection* (Andrews McMeel Publishing, 2019).
2. Truth and Reconciliation Commission of South Africa, *Truth and Reconciliation Commission of South Africa Report*, vols. 1–5 (The Commission, 1998).

Practice the Communal Heart in Dialogue

1. Awareness initiates change. This is the hallmark of the paradoxical nature of change: "Change occurs when one becomes what he is, not when he tries to become what he is not." Arnold R. Beisser, "The Paradoxical Theory of Change," *Gestalt Journal* 1, no. 1 (1970): 77–80.

Chapter 10: A Reunion We Long For

Epigraph: Carl G. Jung, *Psychology and Religion: West and East*, trans. R. F. C. Hull (Princeton University Press, 1969).

1. Iain McGilchrist attributes the parable of the Master and His Emissary to Friedrich Nietzsche, though he notes that he is not certain of its source.
2. "Basic trust," a term introduced by Erik Erikson, refers to the early-formed sense that life is dependable, relationships are safe, and the world can be met with openness rather than fear. Erik H. Erikson, *Childhood and Society* (W. W. Norton & Company, 1950).

Chapter 11: The Third Way Opens a New Path

Epigraph: Jalal-al-Din Rumi, *The Essential Rumi*, trans. Coleman Barks (Harper One, 1995).

1. Sometimes the force initiating change is called the "affirming force."
2. Some authors, including myself, see the Law of Three as mirroring what has been referred to as the "McGilchrist Manueuvre," explained in Chapter 5. The right hemisphere initiates with a felt sense of the whole, while the left hemisphere focuses on details, categorizes them, and then gathers them into the right hemisphere, where they are accepted into a new Gestalt or rejected. And the process starts all over again. The Fourth Way, "Paradise Lost

Twice," *The Fourth Way's Substack*, Substack, November 25, 2025, https://thefourthway.substack.com/p/paradise-lost-twice.

3. The "Law of Three" is a foundational concept in the teachings of G.I. Gurdjieff, a spiritual teacher and mystic whose work significantly influenced the Enneagram, integrative psychology, and contemplative traditions. The Law of Three states, "Every phenomenon arises from the interplay of three forces: the affirming, the denying, and the reconciling." P.D. Ouspensky, *In Search of the Miraculous: Fragments of an Unknown Teaching* (Harcourt, 1949); Cynthia Bourgeault, *The Holy Trinity and the Law of Three: Discovering the Radical Truth at the Heart of Christianity* (Shambhala Publications, 2013).
4. Some philosophers, like Hanzi Freinacht, have begun to call the next cultural epoch "metamodernism," a term used to describe the synthesis that emerges after modernity and postmodernity.
5. Ken Wilber's integrative approach builds on the developmental framework of Spiral Dynamics (Beck and Cowan, 1996), synthesizing Clare Graves's original research (2005) into a broader AQAL model of human and cultural evolution (Wilber, 2000, 2006). Don Edward Beck and Christopher C. Cowan, *Spiral Dynamics: Mastering Values, Leadership and Change* (Blackwell Publishing, 1996); Clare Graves, *The Never-Before-Published Works of Clare W. Graves: Levels of Human Existence* (ECLET Publishing, 2005); Ken Wilber, *A Theory of Everything: An Integral Vision for Business, Politics, Science, and Spirituality* (Shambhala Publications, 2000); Ken Wilber, *Integral Spirituality: A Startling New Role for Religion in the Modern and Postmodern World* (Integral Books, 2006).
6. British pediatrician and psychoanalyst Donald Winnicott called "good enough mothers" caregivers who do not need to be perfect, but who are consistently attuned, responsive, and capable of repairing ruptures in connection. Donald W. Winnicott, "Transitional Objects and Transitional Phenomena," *International Journal of Psycho-Analysis* 34 (1953): 89–97.
7. While these are my observations, they were made recently public in "The Psychological Drivers of the Metacrisis: Daniel Schmatchenberger, Iain McGilchrist, John Vervaeke," The Consilience Project, posted on December 2023, YouTube video, 3:21:54, https://www.youtube.com/watch?v=-6V0qmDZ2gg.
8. In Jungian psychology, chaos and order are often viewed as symbolic expressions of the feminine and masculine archetypes, not in terms of gender, but as universal principles that exist within each individual and in the

collective psyche. C. G. Jung, *The Archetypes and the Collective Unconscious*, 2nd ed. (Routledge, 1991).

Chapter 12: The Dynamic Reality of Belonging

Epigraph: Hanzi Freinacht, *The Listening Society: A Metamodern Guide to Politics* (Metamoderna, 2017).

1. A foundational study demonstrated that carbon and nutrients can be transferred between different tree species via mycorrhizal networks, highlighting the cooperative and communicative nature of forest ecosystems. Suzanne W. Simard, David A. Perry, et al., "Net Transfer of Carbon Between Tree Species with Shared Ectomycorrhizal Fungi," *Nature* 388, no. 6642 (1997): 579–582.
2. South Africa's first Black president, Nelson Mandela, prioritized national unity by establishing the Truth and Reconciliation Commission (TRC) in 1995. Chaired by Archbishop Desmond Tutu, the TRC provided a platform for victims and perpetrators of apartheid-era crimes to share their experiences, promoting healing through truth-telling and amnesty. This restorative justice model emphasized the African philosophy of *ubuntu* (I am because We are), highlighting shared humanity and interconnectedness. Mandela's philosophy of forgiveness resonated worldwide, influencing leaders and communities grappling with histories of conflict and injustice. His legacy underscores the power of compassion and understanding in overcoming deep-seated divisions. Truth and Reconciliation Commission of South Africa, *Truth and Reconciliation Commission of South Africa Report* (Macmillan Reference, 1998).

Chapter 13: Circles of Renewal

Epigraph: Margaret Mead (attributed), *Earth at Omega: Passage to Planetization*, ed. Donald Keys (Branden Press, 1982).

1. A rhizome is a type of plant root system—like ginger, bamboo, or crabgrass—that spreads horizontally, nonhierarchically, and in multiple directions at once and has been used as a concept for describing how systems grow and connect. Gilles Deleuze and Félix Guattari, *A Thousand Plateaus: Capitalism and Schizophrenia* (University of Minnesota Press, 1987).

2. The phrase "islands of coherence," or more specifically, "small islands of coherence," is widely attributed to complexity theorist Ilya Prigogine though the exact source of the quotation is difficult to verify.
3. In Stephen M. R. Covey, *The Speed of Trust: The One Thing That Changes Everything* (Simon and Schuster, 2006), Covey observed that when trust is high, productivity moves faster and with less effort. The same is true in the relational field: Trust acts as the invisible connective tissue that allows flow, repair, and coherence to emerge.
4. A group of up to seven participants balances diversity of input with relational coherence. As group size increases, the number of possible interpersonal relationships expands rapidly according to the formula n(n-1)/2. So, a group of seven people contains twenty-one distinct relational connections requiring attention and coordination. Richard D.Bartlett, "Five Scales of Microsolidarity," https://www.microsolidarity.cc.
5. Collective intelligence refers to a group's capacity to perform a wide range of tasks effectively, exceeding what would be predicted by the intelligence or expertise of individual members alone. Research suggests that groups with a higher proportion of women tend to demonstrate greater collective intelligence than mixed-gender groups or male-only groups. This advantage is largely attributed to higher average social sensitivity and more equal participation among group members, factors that predicted group performance more strongly than participants' individual IQs. The study does not claim that women as individuals are more intelligent, nor that all-female groups outperform mixed groups. Rather, it shows that the presence of women increased the likelihood of relational conditions, social sensitivity, and equitable turn-taking, which enables collective intelligence to emerge. Anita Williams Woolley, Christopher F. Chabris, Alex Pentland, Nada Hashmi, and Thomas W. Malone, "Evidence for a collective intelligence factor in the performance of human groups," *Science* 330, no. 6004 (2010): 686–688.

   These findings, taken together with those obtained by Stoet and Geary (2018), suggest that gender differences may reflect complementary orientations: differences in interest and attention shaped by both biology and culture, which, when integrated rather than flattened, enhance collective functioning. Gijsbert Stoet and David C. Geary, "The Gender-Equality Paradox in Science, Technology, Engineering, and Mathematics Education," *Psychological Science* 29, no. 4 (February 2018): 581–593.
6. Rosa Parks was a civil rights activist best known for her pivotal role in the Montgomery Bus Boycott. On December 1, 1955, in Montgomery,

Alabama, she, a Black woman, refused to give up her seat to a white passenger on a segregated bus. Her courageous act of resistance sparked a year-long boycott of the city's bus system, becoming a powerful symbol of dignity and nonviolent protest against racial injustice.

7. Peter M. Senge, *The Fifth Discipline: The Art and Practice of the Learning Organization* (Doubleday, 1990).
8. Otto Scharmer, *Theory U: Leading from the Future as It Emerges*, 2nd ed. (Berrett-Koehler Publishers, 2016).

Chapter 14: From One Light Come Many Rays of Hope

Epigraph: Thich Nhat Hanh (attributed), *The Heart of the Buddha's Teaching: Transforming Suffering into Peace, Joy, and Liberation* (Broadway Books, 1998).

Chapter 15: An Emergent Movement Gathering Life

Epigraph: Unknown (n.d.), "Alone, we can go fast. Together, we can go far" (African proverb).

1. Thomas MacManus and Tony Ward, "Utopia in the Midst of Dystopia? The Peace Community of San José de Apartadó," *Justice, Power & Resistance* 3, no. 1 (2016): 217–239, https://www.european-group.org/wp-content/uploads/2024/06/MacManus-and-Ward-2016-Utopia-in-the-Midst-of-Dystopia-The-Peace-Community-of-San-Jose-de-Apartado.pdf.
2. Gwen Burnyeat, "'Rupture' and the State: The 'Radical Narrative' of the Peace Community of San José de Apartadó, Colombia," *Antípoda: Revista de Antropología y Arqueología* 29 (2017): 17–40.
3. Audrey Tang and E. Glen Weyl, *Plurality: The Future of Collaborative Technology and Democracy* (RadicalxChange Press, 2023). Tang encourages us to think relationally and to move from thinking of an "internet of things" to an "internet of beings," from "virtual reality" to a "shared reality," from "machine learning" to "collaborative learning," and from "user experience" to "human experience."
4. Jigsaw, "What Could BG Be? Enabling a Large-Scale Conversation in Kentucky," *Medium*, February 14, 2025, https://medium.com/jigsaw/what-could-bg-be-enabling-a-large-scale-conversation-in-kentucky-70071f4fe268; "*Government Technology News*", Govtech.com. Launched in 2025, this

month-long online conversation invited residents of Warren County to collaboratively envision the community's future. The initiative utilized the Polis platform, developed by the Computational Democracy Project, and was supported by Jigsaw (a unit within Google) and Innovation Engine. The project aimed to gather diverse perspectives to inform the BG 2050 vision document, which will guide the region's growth over the next twenty-five years. This approach exemplifies distributive democracy by actively involving citizens in decision-making processes.

5. *San Francisco Standard*, "First Look: Inside Frontier San Francisco, the City's First 'Vertical Village,'" May 18, 2025.

Epilogue: It Starts with Us

Epigraph: Alice Walker, *We Are the Ones We Have Been Waiting For: Inner Light in a Time of Darkness* (New Press, 2006).

ABOUT THE AUTHOR

Author photo by Heidi Breuner

CLAUDIA DOMMASCHK is a licensed Marriage and Family Therapist (LMFT) based in Northern California. In addition to her full-time psychotherapy practice, she is a long-time student of Gestalt Practice, the writer of *Immediacy Forum* on Substack, an international executive coach, and a community weaver exploring the path of relational healing in a time of profound transition.

As the familiar structures of modern life continue to unravel, many are awakening to a deeper longing for connection, coherence, and meaning. Claudia's work centers on the belief that this liminal space between what was and what is emerging holds immense possibilities. She invites us to slow down, turn toward what is real, and cultivate the relational intelligence needed to meet this cultural threshold through presence, care, and a shared willingness to evolve together.